Smarter Phoneless

SEAN P. DWYER

Cover design by Samuel Pliszka
Cover photo of bus taken by Kacie Dwyer

Printed in the United States of America

First Edition, 2020

ISBN: 978-1-7321286-2-0

This book is available at a wholesale discount by specific request. For inquiries and other comments regarding the text or author, send an email to
universityandgoodman@gmail.com

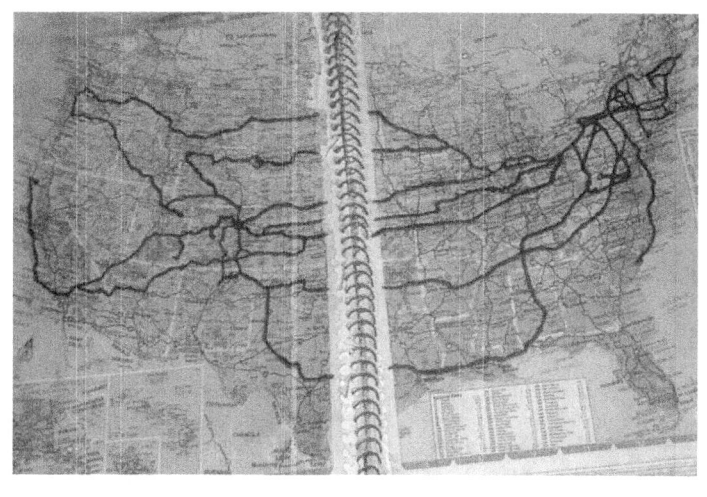

Also by Sean P. Dwyer:

To Accept a Wooden Nickel
Sometimes They Smile

Smarter Phoneless

introduction

The last day of July, 2019

The bus wasn't running, it was flying as the two of us crossed the Massachusetts state line to New York along one of America's many glorious scenic byways. My sister Kacie occupied the co-pilot seat, following a paper map and magnetic compass, directing me across old Route 2. Just barely ahead of schedule, we kept away from Interstate-90 from western Massachusetts to Troy, staying north and roughly parallel to it through the mountainous backroads of the Berkshires.

It was there!

Here!

Somewhere after the center roads tightened and opened up again past the city of Troy: *Dibble*.

The only association I had with Troy at the time was him, my old friend, one of inimitable character-truth, always such a joyous thrill to correspond with. Kacie and I passed right through a tight downtown Troy, keeping on Route 2 until crossing a bridge that pointed at Schenectady. We were looking for Route 20, another majestic road that connected the Atlantic and Pacific, predating the current interstate system and serving as an intercontinental byway before toll roads and trite thruways laced the country.

I was hunched over at the wheel slightly with eyes fixated at street signs ahead when Dibble's burgundy Pontiac Vibe fell into my line of vision, him sailing up that left lane and beeping his horn repeatedly after realizing that in the mystery bus passing by his local gym was his old friend. For him, it was just his lunch break and another day spent in the moment.

These were slim circumstances. By then he knew that I had been working on converting an old school bus, but had no idea what it looked like. There was also no indication from us that we would be passing through. Somehow the world was still small enough for us to strangely cross paths again.

As he trailed me through a number of congested traffic junctions, I hastily pulled into a grocery store parking lot. When Dibble got out of his car, I cut the rumbling engine of the bus and leapt through the air-doors that hissed as I flipped the switch and the pressure released.

I noticed his sideburns reaching past his earlobes. His striped shirt was tucked in, revealing the baggy black cargo pants that reached and covered the tops of his shiny dress shoes. He had the sharp awareness of a hawk to catch a glimpse of the bus and grab my attention with absolutely no time to spare. How was it even possible that he caught us? How many others would have been caught neck bent, arched down at a pocket computer again instead?

Surely he was someone who liked to keep his head up.

Kacie and I considered and spoke about reaching out to him as we passed by, but decided against it because of timing and the assumption that he was busy, it being midday of a workweek. The two of us were returning from an oceanside road trip to Rhode Island, intending to make it back by the next morning for a work shift of hers in our home city of Rochester.

When Kacie asked about how his job was going, Dibble raised an eyebrow. "Installing smart-lights— you heard? All part of the *internet of things*," he explained. When he realized that he had our attention, he continued. "It's actually a bit..."

"Invasive?" I returned after his short pause.

"Syracuse and Buffalo are already live with these systems," Dibble said.

"And what happens if a city decides to oppose a system such as this?"

"They have no choice—the old light systems are outdated and will soon fail."

These light systems, capable of picking up on distressful street side signals like gunshots and shrieks, are built in with features to tune in, listen, and track on command. What does this mean? In an effort to deliver public safety, have we effectively agreed to let technocratic systems wiretap entire cities?

After Dibble departed, Kacie was thrown off. She was uncertain as to why he thought and acted the way he did, and in so had no explanation for his madness. Meanwhile, intersubjectivity was at work. For just a moment I felt the sentience of myself, all in line with everything else that thought attracts. When I realized that even Dibble could be mistaken for being insensible, I was left with a chill.

part one

SMARTER PHONELESS

1

How about that moment
when the eyes of the passerby
lock with your own—
a reminder of inner immortality,
in recognition of the beauty
that will soon pass
like all else in our lives

When in the eyes of the passerby
you see yourself
but not the self of that moment,
a self from another time, another stage, another land

It's true—you're both thinking the same thing
if not, those eyes wouldn't be so bright
eager to share a story
and their hat wouldn't sit so perfectly on their head
like you wore it one day

When you lock eyes with that passerby
you remember to give them that look,
because you know that someday you will get it in
return
and that surely someday there will be peace
again.

what is a straight forward narrative?
what is spontaneous prose?
o to reach for the unrestricted
a new renaissance
active screen free living
in preference of the tangible

> *kindled five senses*
> *leading along*

potential abounds as I soar,
burdens shrinking in rear-view

Like the last few popcorn kernels
burrowed at bottom of hot bag—
eventually the first few pop, under enough force,
before more follow and set the norm
but no matter the pressure and stress applied,
there are always outliers at the bottom
fully understanding how to overcome, master,
remain true.
Could popcorn kernels resemble
the free-thinkers of the world?
This is classic Dr. Bobism.

Like the dirty travelers
in forest green overalls
knew so well
as they bit into uncut watermelon,
hitching to Rainbow:
where there is great love there are always miracles!

There is a trail to certainty
a reason to resist complacency
like a big metal key on your coffee table

it is there if you are willing to take it.

Whether the key leads inside or out
it must lead somewhere!
With that key must come trust,
as trust is key, and virtue ennobles.

Before I left the house I grabbed a pen from a table
initially indistinguishable
from the one in my pocket usually
it was a bold .10 thickness rather than my usual .07,
and the clip was missing
as if it had covered a few miles
before my seeing feeling writing.

It felt lighter that day,
less pressure to release the ink—

Don't you know that what ceases to make it to paper is
but a thought wandering through time, just waiting to
be caught by hand and placed onto a plot of time's
crazy book of memories?

2

I look to wonderous, borderless nature when unsure

From a very young age
I wandered about my backyard,
my earliest memories
endless and primitive
It was...Kindergarten

When I was four years old, my family obtained a
beautiful ranch on an edge in which American
suburban development met primitive forest. In my
case, this was Webster, New York.

The only signs of man past the edge of where
my dad stopped mowing the lawn and where the forest
started were a handful of tattered chicken coops
abandoned deep in the woods, along with an old car
half-returned to nature's green arms. There was an old
farm stretching across the other side of the street, but
our side remained endless. The many plants, creatures,
and trees dominated the land. I remember my dad
leading me on an exploration of these paths on foot,
and later by golf cart. There was no sense of a property
line or border—instead, just ideas of the unknown set a
dynamic edge.

This is all faint, before much of the land (aside from a
few acres that remained ours) was sold over to a friend
of family, a homebuilder that turned the acreage into a
winding neighborhood of homes constructed along the

lucky trees and manmade ponds that endured the build.

I recall watching the land evolve as I grew up. Lots and lines drawn, carved plots empty and desolate after the trees were cleared and before houses were put up. One time I was fooling around with my cousins and blasted a rock through the glass of a giant bulldozer that was parked back there. It wasn't an act of protest against them or anything, as I was too young to have any interest in objecting to what was going on. I didn't feel that it was a problem that the nature of my backyard was dwindling or anything like that. I even felt guilt when I threw the rock through the bulldozer's window and didn't mention it to my parents for years.

Throughout my childhood, I was fortunate enough to feed my wandering spirit as I met friends and stuck with family that led me through their backyards that were mystical like this but in their own way, of course. From golf courses after-hours to corn fields and wedges of wilderness like the one between my later home and the Irondequoit Bay, it was always a joy to reach for and immerse myself in the next extraordinary landscape.

The front lines of a modernizing world
all as wild as prehistoric America,
all as wild as tomorrow's America

We found the boundary,
reaching for what we once couldn't civilize
the worst mistake is to believe the dotted lines

The transaction to sell the additional land away did not ruin the wildness of that house, it created a new wildness. We spent many hours running around outside, climbing trees, and making forts and hideouts out of what we found. But at the same time, we were witnessing a cycle. I grew familiar with land being sold over and subdivided in order to take new forms faster than I could grow up.

When we returned to Webster
months after our long hitchhiking trip
Dibble drove me to the front lines
(forest of his youth)
showing off the dreadful sight:
land half-ripped apart,
marked with property lines to-be

we set up chairs,
played on our guitars facing the site.
Deforestation blues, we called it

when a homeowner caught sight, approached,

"don't worry,
we'll be gone with the trees

the new lines will become,
the new houses will be built,"
and now they are.

o precious pines!
robustly you will return

3

July, 2014
Along the edge of Commerce City, Colorado,
traveling East.

Dibble and I had been away from our Upstate New
York lives for thirty-five days by then, already having
logged over 5,000 miles by hitchhiking, on our way
back to complete the loop and return home. There
were tokens of keepsake and memories gathered,
compiling as we learned methods of drifting as we
went along. Friends were made across each passing
city. It was easy—people with thrill in their eyes were
easy to find, ready to share their treasured stories and
give us their best impressions of the small towns and
big cities that were all new to us and regular to them.

Stealth camping in vineyards,
                            sanctuaries,
                                    fields,

making friends with the world,
no matter the flash of city lights
or vast vacant stretches of country
unafraid of the homeless,
multi-day stretches of all-foot-travel
nights in Chicago
turned around at Chinatown
overnight rides through Montana
sleeping beneath the space needle

                no tent
                        just dark sky

Phones—
they really did us little help on the road

More often, they seemed to distract us from catching
the fine details of each place we passed through, even
though it displayed our location on a map and claimed
to connect us with the world.

In an effort to cross a busy, multi-lane highway
in Commerce City, my smartphone slipped out of my
pocket and into a sewer trench, never to be seen again.
It was a complete accident.

After the initial panic of losing photographs and
contacts, an odd lightness followed.

Dibble's phone was avoided from the very
beginning of our trip, and fittingly became useless by
the time we reached day 20 and Seattle. But in
Commerce City, a few weeks later, the two of us were
finally both left without pocket computers of our own
to assist us.

There was something happening that was
larger than us—something tranquil in each hint of air
and sight of strangeness. Even before the drop, there
were feelings of weariness with screens. We
considered it cheating to use such a device to find a
ride. If anything, it was the complacency that was
attached to them that frustrated and drove us out of
New York in the first place. We were in search of the
mad, the actual mad, concentrated on harvesting the
excitement of our surroundings, and in doing so looked
West, following rumored lures and chasing what was
unknown.

I did not realize all of this right away. Maybe it
was old news for Dibble, already possessing a confident

grip on this. Oftentimes, I still found myself caught up in heavy, muddy thought. On the other hand, Dibble was keen and had a knack for precisely pointing out troubles of device overuse, urging me to turn it off and see the world. I believed what he was saying but still sometimes stubbornly defended the other side. Even so, there was no denying what I felt. These outlooks of mine quietly grew each time I kept it away.

It was this sequence of events in Commerce City that carried me—losing the link was absolutely worth it. Without it, the importance of each object on hand was transformed. More so, each interaction with a new stranger became the next important moment to connect and gather local insight, acting as a director to the next destination. Despite an absence of GPS, travel became more fluid when it shifted to exclusive face-to-face interactions along each town that we reached next. After only a few interactions, it became clear that we could make better time without them. Even when we didn't, life was simply more fun when we took up the simple change of habit.

I peer back at this breakthrough to freedom with merit. The subtraction of a phone from my life opened up a world of new color—anything was possible. No one could take away the feeling. With it, we continued building on an idea that quickly took its own form. With no device to retreat to, emotions as they unfold are given the space they need to sink in properly, becoming stronger and more definite. In turn, the sincerity of the world surfaces.

4

June, 2014
Keeping on the topic of the first hitchhiking trip

"Today, we are born."

I was eighteen. Dibble was nineteen.
It was our first attempt to reach the faraway western coast.

In a certain way, it felt a lot like stepping into a world of blind chance. Meanwhile, I still had a prompt lifeline to resort to, full of support and quick fallbacks in case anything was to go wrong.

But it was still the road, the rough road. The effort of defying what was normal expanded my general comfort with my surroundings as we succeeded, allowing purpose to shine through coincidence. Details, minute on the surface, acted like doors and told so much once I was willing to open them.

We left New York in search of the timeless American Dream. As far as I knew, it *was* blind chance what would happen, although we had an idea of what we wanted to find, and in so decided it was worth it to grapple to the slim chance we had of getting there. It was after completing my first year of college that I returned to Rochester and linked back up with Dibble for this trip. In only a matter of days, the two of us went from making the decision to leave to beginning the quest. We were unhappy with the mundane state of the people around us, and knew of no better way to stir things up than to flee.

But even in our mutual madness, our circumstances were very different. Notably it was my mother who drove us to the west side of Rochester and dropped us off along a busy highway to begin our pursuit. Meanwhile, it was Dibble's parents who were entirely unaware of our plans to leave the state and begin hitchhiking for Chicago. Instead of letting them know, a handwritten note was left on his parents' bedside before we left that explained our intentions.

Due to our differing positions leading up to the trip, along with jointly experiencing the natural thrills of an unfolding America in front of our eyes, our outlook on the smartphones we brought along soon became extraordinary. As my family wished me fortunate travels and awaited personal updates from my smartphone, Dibble avoided his device at all costs and reminded me to put the screen away. For a while I thought my phone would do us well—keep us safe, help us get our word out, and allow for outsiders to follow our journey. Could I have been more wrong?

Good is everywhere,
will only manifest where let to grow.

From very early on, this issue created jealousy and separation between Dibble and I. In the midst of exciting roadside encounters, a wall was slowly, steadily being built between the two of us. As he ignored his family ties back east and gazed upon the vast West with little concern for his phone, I gazed too but was quick to defend my smartphone and pull for it when unsure, looking to it for answers. This surely bred discontent from Dibble, feeding the passion he already had to reach and grab for a life uninvolved with screens.

It was an accident that my iPhone escaped from me during an attempt to cross a busy highway in Commerce City, Colorado. The crossover soon left me convinced beyond belief in what I was already beginning to suspect.

5

October, 2018

Over the years, I have gone back and forth between carrying a flip phone and living with no screen at all. At one point I even offered handyman services from an office phone hooked up to a mobile hot spot. A recent flip phone of mine was shut off unexpectedly, due to my carrier permanently terminating 3G access in my area.

After a trip to a phone store, the alternative they offered me was a new 4G flip phone for an equally expensive cost (ouch—especially for a flimsy thing that looked no different than many other flips I have owned in the past). Of course, they brought up the other option of purchasing a basic, "entry-level" smartphone designed for people like me, reluctant to fall in line with the devices of the changing times.

I wish not to attack any individual in my life or in the world, but rather acknowledge a multifaceted, widespread issue that I have struggled to explain and cope with for years.

Consider the following:

--It is has been admitted and is now widely accepted that these devices in their totality provide us with short dopamine rewards that keep us hooked to screens and mistrusting others. It is no secret that a large percentage of the population cannot imagine a world without daily doses of screen time.

--Many public spaces are now dominated by phoners of all ages. Will the harms ever outweigh the benefits for these brothers and sisters, friends and strangers? Pokémon Go, location-tracking snapchat features, and many other augmented reality applications popular with young people worry me as I watch them wander around, staring through their phones like sleepwalkers along the bright grass. We have all seen it. Who will take action?

--Personal robot servants have entered our homes and have become normalized (Alexa, Echo, Siri). Walk into any American home and call for their name and chances are high that some sort of robot will chime in and offer service. How long will it take before they grow legs, start preparing our meals, and learn to keep our houses clean? Privacy concerns are widespread in regards to the information that these devices collect and what companies can do with these massive databases of sensitive material.

--Big tech companies have recently shown American citizens, loud and clear, that they are in control of what is allowed on social media newsfeeds (Does free speech fly on the internet? Where is the Internet Bill of Rights?). They outright ban individuals that post or share "untrustworthy" or "hateful" information, push undesirable opinions to the bottom of newsfeeds, and let users think that their posts are reaching others, but in fact are not (shadow banning).

--People have reported a force that pulls them to their devices, even when it doesn't ring and is across the room. This is dependency! This is no different than drug or food cravings, although the most fanatic users can get away with never confronting the possibility of harmful overuse, and even be rewarded financially for sitting on one relentlessly.

Being removed from major social media platforms means being locked out of the dominant modern idea sharing network that is the internet. As individuals grow more and more dependent on these devices, it will only become more of a shock to be locked out of them. Currently, this is an unregulated catastrophe that will only lead to more problems and more distance between the politically "correct" and "incorrect".

How do we know where Facebook places posts on other newsfeeds? Who is in control of determining what is hateful and unworthy of accessibility? Who is in control of shadow banning? Algorithms, to an extent, people answer, although thousands of humans actually decide this, monitoring the internet as their full-time job.

People want to and are beginning to limit their device use, although through the lens of their systems, you could never tell.

Still, most children have no example of *anyone*, in popular culture or in their own circle, to look up to as someone who lives without one. The dreariest thing is when I see kids too young to even desire this life watch their parents distract themselves for minutes, *HOURS*, uninterrupted, never picking up their head to acknowledge the creation in front of them. For this reason, I do not wonder why children beg for their own years before they understand what they really are.

On the surface, it is undoubtedly a disadvantage to live without a pocket computer in a world that expects to reach you at all hours of the day at any instant. The last thing I want is to be viewed as selfish for distancing myself from owning one of these dangerous devices. If we can look past the surface-level setbacks, rich advantages of stepping back begin to emerge.

At the least, I hope to reserve the right to coexist in a world that is rapidly evolving to require one. In doing so, I strive to provide people with a living example that living screen-free can still be done.

6

January, 2019
Rochester, New York

Dear Mr. John Dwyer (*President of Cricket Wireless*),

I am writing you concerning a unique sponsorship opportunity for Cricket Wireless.

As America narrows in on complete smartphone dependency, it may feel natural to ignore their dark setbacks and the fact that they are now virtually mandatory in modern society. It is a choice of mine to lead by example in abstaining from smartphone ownership. I strive to be living proof that it can still be done with ease and enjoyment.

Smartphone abuse will become a worldwide public health crisis if we do nothing to spread awareness about their dangers. Look around, I am sure that you have taken notice. The wave of smartphone obsession has successfully swept across the world and is not limited to age, demographic, or socio-economic status.

Just in the past decade, we have let these devices slide so deeply into our lives that they are not only acceptable but *encouraged* in classrooms, at dinner tables, in the middle of corporate meetings, and in the hands of our youngest children. Smartphone advertisements are littered across billboards, television advertisements, fast food containers, retail stores, and public transportation signs, convincing us that they must be worth the price. But are the devices really helping us succeed and prosper?

When your child sees you on your phone, they do not realize that you are just replying to an important work email, or learning from a google search. They are reminded that in that moment, the phone was more important to you than them. After only a few observances, it is no surprise that children, just wanting to emulate their loved ones, will demand a pocket screen of their own.

I believe that there is a time and a place to use the internet. But when it is condensed and refined to fit in our pockets, something changes. When the public stopped deciding to spend any time away from their devices, new trends were created. Society shaped itself around the assumption that everyone has their smartphone on their person at all times. This is leading to a dangerously low demand for simple tools, as the smartphone completely replaced potentially life-saving items like the flashlight and the map. Of course, traditional taxi services are on their way to becoming a relic of the past. Even hotel keys are being replaced by apps. Public services will continue to develop around this mold, covertly leaving people out who choose to abstain from screens once they leave their home.

I am here to keep us from forgetting to teach our children to write with a pen, and to help them learn from the natural, tangible world first-hand. It is so important to teach them to enjoy time spent screen-free.

With a smartphone, your eggs are in one basket. If it malfunctions or goes missing, it leaves you without a tool that our brain learns to depend on, it acting as an extension of our memory, a distraction to avoid eye contact and pass time, and an excuse to be ill-prepared. When you leave your device at home, it is much more important to know where you are driving, to do your research before speaking out, and to interact with people with an active mind.

The last time I owned a smartphone dates back to 2014 (I am not elderly or an infant). Since then, I have gone through flip phones, a landline, and periods of nothing. Life was dandy until one day in October of 2018, when it stopped sending and receiving calls and texts. After a trip to a local store, I learned that it had been rendered useless and outdated, kicked off indefinitely from my network. If nothing is done, I worry that simple flip phones will soon become extinct across all carriers.

I dread losing the choice to opt out of smartphone ownership. In the heat of the moment, I chose instead to switch my old cell number over to an office phone. There are surface-level setbacks, but each time I run into a difficult situation, I feel the priceless benefits as I am led to think for myself or ask strangers around me for assistance.

People are curious—questioning their smartphones and the possibility of an alternative, inspired by the idea of freeing up hours of each day to chase their passions instead of getting lost in endless, untrustworthy streams of clutter and empty hope. Is that news to you or does this sound familiar?

I look now to Cricket to inquire for sponsorship. This is a chance to take a step in the right direction, during a time in which major phone companies are continuing to ignore a growing plea for people to take a step back, simplify, and take a stand for the welfare of humankind.

Of all major phone carriers, Cricket is already well known for prepaid plans and simple flip phone deals. If you are interested, this can be a step towards establishing yourselves as the premier flip phone choice—a trustworthy, humanistic choice.

In the end we all prefer the tangible, but through the lens of a screen, you would not be able to tell.

Hope this finds you well,
Sean P. Dwyer

7

December, 2018

Spring was still far away but we were racing into the prime of our lives, building up assets, trying to ready up a crew for summer travels in a school bus. Sadly, Cricket probably preferred the world we knew, so I left them alone after receiving no response from Mr. Dwyer.

2002 Bluebird International 3800 DT466E

We picked it up in Ohio
plain December school day
Strongsville bus garage
$1700 and the man handed over the keys
that one!
the one marked number 95

We had no real mechanic with us but had no choice but to take it when it started up in the lot. The yellow exterior, stop sign still wired in, and eleven rows of seats were enough for the three of us to blend in with the afternoon Ohio traffic and the other fleets of school buses on the roads.

"What do you mean check it out? It's yours— you paid for it, take it."

Right on through Cleveland and back to New York we cruised that bus. I rode along, letting Bowes drive, while Sam tailed us with my truck. It would have been nice if we had a grand place to bring it to and park, but that wasn't in the cards and instead we had to come up with different arrangements for its placement. Bowes backed it right into our narrow strip of driveway between two old Victorian homes in downtown Rochester.

"We're not going to talk about politics, the Super Bowl, or the State of the Union—instead we'll be talking about great jazz music. As you know, in this modern world, we can be heard anywhere in the country, even the world, and can be found online, on your smartphone, tablet, or whatever device you use…"

But I was not complacent

sitting in the minority
arguing to express the difference
between a pocket computer
and a desktop
the latter left at home—
or open for public use at a library.

I felt harms of overload
overlooked, subverted—
the option to unplug
the choice to unplug
demonized

next time you fill out a form
try leaving out your phone number

But we had a bus
        people all around were charged with hope

8

From our house in Rochester to a warehouse in Fairport to the hills that overlook Honeoye Lake, the bus was constantly on the move as we began the first stages of its renovation. Nonetheless, it wasn't until we brought it to Youngstown, New York that we decided to spend the night on it.

This was all following a late arrival to Youngstown, where the massive vehicle sat and waited at Mr. Snell's house along the ice-cold Canadian border. The Niagara River flowed just across the street, in sight from the driver seat of the bus as it towered over the bleak cliffside.

Evan joined Sam and I for extra warmth, temperatures reaching no higher than 10 degrees outside but much warmer within the walls of the bus. We cooked breakfast the next morning on my little camp stove before John, Bowes, Mark, and Steve joined us for an afternoon of planning and acting. We gutted what was left inside, taking out scraps of remaining rubber flooring, detaching heaters, spray painting rust damage inside and outside, and finally caulking holes in the subfloor as we prepared to seal everything off and install floating tongue and groove flooring.

I've hitchhiked the lonely streets of country between Rochester and Youngstown twice before. Now with the bus on the west corner of the state it seemed a little closer to home, one long road connecting the path between the vehicle and my hometown.

We were surrounded by doubt, but my friends were ready to find out where the project could lead. Bowes enjoyed the art of labor and applying hard skills to get work done, but would he embrace a gritty, bohemian life that the bus would soon offer? He could undoubtedly become the on-site mechanic, naturally rising to the front of the line to care for each nut and bolt in ways that others just didn't grasp. Bowes also saw the troubles and dangers of the smartphone in ways I wished others were sometimes more willing to. All I wanted was to keep people from turning a blind eye to their apparent dangers. Why was their convenience so worth defending?

There was entertaining talk about implementing a box for smartphones to be dropped into upon entry to the bus. May the bus be a temple for mindfulness, purposeful action, interaction!

I feared being outvoted. I supposed that we were so close as a group because of our moments away from the screens, but as the bus manifested, our foundations were being stripped away. It did not come from hours a day of screen use, wake to night buzzing and phony, faceless networking. It came from periods of silent contemplation, freeing and slowing of minds in order to create manifestations of visions that were initially unclear but in hindsight timeless. It took many moments of leaving everything behind and hitting the road, only to find that letting go was what brought the fruits of necessity. Higher order gets involved when control is surrendered.

It felt too natural to hesitate regarding the welfare of the group, so much so that letting go brought relief. I was confident that things would open up again as our lease in Rochester concluded.

True spirit comes and goes

returning after deserting
resembling the changing seasons
never complacent but altogether flowing
following everlasting forms

I must not forget that I am not alone,
but so often it feels it when blocks go up
and friends reject compassion
as it stands in front of them

As our bubble pops
and the people disperse
I wonder what will ripple and what will be lost

True stillness is nearly unreachable
will you be the blade of grass or the wind that bends it?

9

"Smartphones? Waste of precious breath! Opt-out, you're smarter phoneless!"

Many people are disgruntled by the state of current events, confused by chosen talking points in politics and under the impression that we are being distracted. Well, distracted from what?

Half of me was dying to stand up and interrupt my sister's a capella competition with an announcement of this sort, an opportune moment to reach hundreds of individuals packed into the University of Rochester's auditorium to snap photos and videos of their kids, sacrificing precious moments of the show to watch it through a screen instead of with their naked eyes.

After Kacie's performance, she explained her group's moments of chaos between songs. They attempted to use a smartphone as opposed to a traditional pitch pipe to harmonize and find their starting note before starting the next song. Of course, the app failed to deliver in the moment and, unknowingly to us in the audience, they were forced to start on the wrong pitch anyway.

Just weeks before the competition, I presented her a flip phone for Christmas to switch to in exchange for her current device. After initially expressing excitement for it, she decided to fall back on the switch and keep her iPhone. Perhaps if she had made the switch, the group would have felt her ripple and acted to move away from smartphone reliance for their performance. But instead, an example was made of their dangerous features and deceptive impressions of helpfulness, failing to be as dependable as their single-use, traditional alternative tools.

I must reiterate that I mean no disrespect to my peers and loved ones. I just wondered how long it would take before somebody decided that they were just not worth it anymore. I struggled to stand with my contemporaries that agreed with me on the topic but kept from "walking the line" and joining a simple, noble stream of thought. It was already so rare to catch people willingly going as far as removing their smartphone from their life with such reasoning.

Is it worse to knowingly follow along or to live ignorant and blinded alongside of their dangers? It did not take long for me to grow impatient in my efforts to try to convince people that agree but keep from applying the truth to their own life. There was no doubt that they were more aware of the dangers as opposed to someone who had never heard this argument, but it was *so rarely* ever enough for anyone to make such a switch.

10

We mustn't be perfect
but rather just truthful
as we pass on the words
that stuck from youth

How long before spring?
Why, it may never come again
but you better bet until it does
I'll be outside

    running in snow

I was up in Potsdam retreating from Rochester again. An abundant number of individuals with each their own eclectic way of living took the stage for an open mic night at Maxfield's. After trekking through Ives park in white-out conditions to reach Market Street, I took a seat at the end of the bar next to a lady that at first said nothing as she typed away on her laptop.

I didn't say anything until after I ordered my food, a cup of French onion soup that, unknowing to me, matched her order.

"I didn't copy you on purpose!" I said to her as the bartender brought her cup out just a few moments after he took my order, this breaking the silence between the two of us. Me being all shy couldn't pull her out of her laptop quite yet, as she mostly kept typing but replied like a friend would about how soup is an ideal order for such a cold, snowy day.

After my soup arrived, we opened up a bit and talked about schooling, she being a Clarkson student studying something in regards to data and research online—writing a paper detailing her call to regulate the internet from "hate and online trolls". I was mostly silent and attentive as she explained this to the bartender, who I soon found out was her fiancé. Their comments drove me to continue the conversation, me being eager to hear more about how she viewed what she identified as the out-of-control internet. I wondered where she stood on censorship. Did she realize that that she was precisely proposing a halt to free speech online?

She did not close her laptop until things really got going, as another character pulled up a seat at the bar on the other side of her. He looked familiar but I did not realize until he pointed it out that we were in the same biopsychology class a few years ago.

"So what did you specialize in, during your studies of psych?"

I thought for a moment. It had been almost two years since I last sat in a classroom. "Tough to put in words. Wilderness education?"

He was thrown off and wanted more. Izzy, the girl between us, showed interest with her eyes as she also dialed in. "And what do you suppose you'll do with that?"

"Well, I already use it all the time—I'm happiest when I wander amongst wonderful people in big drifts across the country interacting and documenting it all in a pocket book, then typing it up when I get home. Working on another one now..."

People frequently tell me that I should boast more, and maybe I should, but it's a difficult, tender thing to bring up, it entirely shifting how people view and interact with me.

Immediately:

"So, what are your returns?"—

What kind of question was that? He wanted to know about the money before he even heard of what the books were about. In fact, he never asked what they were about. Izzy was excited and intrigued and made me happy that it was brought up. It was enough for her to close her laptop.

People often suggested that I get marketing and find a way to get the word out. Ideally I agreed but at the same time I felt that it would deter me from what inspires my writings—humble spontaneous drifting— and doing networking and marketing on a small scale, with each individual I converse with, face-to-face. Of course, that choice may lead me down a long path, but would I ever prefer it any other way? To shorten the path and fix that, people constantly told me that I should utilize the web. Maybe it would get people to put down the screens, people say, but to me it seemed that I must look in other directions—in fixation of the truth, staring it down, daring it to try to intimidate me. I could never sell out my spirit of savagery.

In an instant I felt the rushing drive to drift again, be it! Worries fade away on the road as daily energy transforms in an effort to resolve the basic needs of my life.

Think long of each item you carry

like each face you find,
they will flash before your eyes
in just a moment's time

enjoy; soon off;

out on their own journey

11

March, 2019

In high regard of paper,
my actions were of the other
filling notebooks with ink
stacking them high so they could be returned to
no matter a battery life or system outdated

On paper, words are safer as they are scribbled
more difficult to modify

On censorship:
it only magnifies extremism
Where do the exiled retreat?
Bradbury would be shocked

After many years of a primitive, wild-west-internet,
censorship online is now routine as major monopoly
media platforms hold (and exercise) the authority to
eliminate entire topics and keywords from returning
search results

moderators chosen
given free power to decide
what is hateful?
what is phony?

When considered dangerous,
users sent packing

thoughts and information removed from the web.

The internet is at risk of ceasing to be a place for all to gather and learn, and instead turning into a place of thought-privilege—abide and you can stay. Even as what is being censored is justified, the act of creating a voiceless list of outcasts is daring. Who shall we choose to judge and decide the fate of every internet user, someone that agrees with me or you?

My thoughts drain of jargon
leaving space for them to grow again—
what a search for the words
to address and impress conflict.
Important debate today?

Independence vanishes without a choice to speak:
let the arguers dispute on all fronts
let the skeptics reach the scientists
maybe then people will not fear being isolated
for being wrong

so why censor opposition
why censor individuals
fighting for voice
fighting for liberty?
I wish for the opposers to debate

Should the misguided be educated or banished?
by denouncing,
the banished will only form their own assembly of
outsiders,
using those actions to attract attention.

A great intellectual battle is here,
a cause sounding for attention

Phony divides keep great minds from
collaborating,
keeping topics in obscurity
that belong in limelight

So why stifle, repress, censor?

There will be no control group—
there will not be a choice

whether or not we would like to turn it off
when it is beaming through windows
via street lights and smart sensors
every street corner,
every roadside

Look outside,
dare to count the towers

find them disguised
fake trees, fake windmills,
painted to match brick and concrete
strapped to water towers and hotels
hospitals and hardware stores
lofty, looming over neighborhoods
joining the scenic highway
and distant hilltop views.

They haven't been there long
seemed to have popped up overnight

Even if they are safe
why so many
How long will they last
before they need to be scrapped and replaced?
Are they recyclable?

Those calling for a green revolution contradict
themselves when they wield their high-tech devices in
the name of the environment. I have been told that the
planet would be so much cleaner if there was no reason
to leave home again. We can upload our lives to the
cloud and never pollute a thing—clutter of the world
would disappear! They claim that artificial intelligence
saves and extends our lives, but disregard that it is the
power of attraction—the unity of inner and outer

wildness—that keeps us fruitful and thirsty to live another day, conscious of our impacts and desires to keep the world healthy and in balance so that it can keep turning.

Have we been tricked?

When we distance ourselves from an issue,
it becomes easier to write off,
leaving our circle,
entering indifference

I'm not saying this is hidden information,
at least The Wall Street Journal covered it
but note this
Bill Clinton made it illegal in 1996,
as he signed the Telecommunications Act into law,
to oppose cell phone tower construction under the basis of environmental effects.

Let that sink in: towns and cities can be sued for deciding to oppose the construction of technology.
As construction continued, I searched the Wall Street Journal each day for new articles to even just mention their dangers. Was I better off disregarding the petitions and yard signs scattering America? I worried that it was too late, especially as I stared at the infrastructure that was already built.

We need space

space to run when nature's urges call;
space to preserve the *option* to run;
forget the digital shackles
remember the freedom of empty pockets
no destination in mind

When my hunter-gatherer spirit fades
decisively I run back for it
and there! it glows again

      Of course,
      these people rarely see newsfeeds

Turning away from society and running is dangerous
—literally and figuratively—
By doing so it tells the world
that you are not content with it,
that you have enough hope to believe
something out there is better off chasing.

Something about my experience of first running away in 2014 feels like it came just in the nick of time. The dodge came during a crossover in mass-thought that was already underway. My experiences struck me so hard that I needed to document them as they unfolded. If I realized any of this any later, I may have never proceeded to start writing it all down as I saw it. I hypothesize that because of the dodge, my opinions were allowed to further move away from the majority, becoming outlandish to many that did not understand why I would ever choose to opt out of a stationary, automated life.

Running away allowed me to focus on why I was frustrated with the world. It allowed me to learn about a side of American culture that classrooms or lecture halls rarely had time for.

I understood the confirmation bias, and paid attention to the hazards of picking and choosing scientific research to cater to my preconceived beliefs. That aside, I am concerned with the evolution of culture that is *following* as stationary automation continues to be favored by the majority. For example, I am familiar with and believe the research that currently states that self-driving cars are safer than human drivers. Meanwhile, I am weary of the social and cultural outcomes that will follow once we give up the skill, forget how to drive, and hand over more control to automation. That does not mean I am ignoring science, or that I disagree. My intention in that regard is to shine light on the repercussions and subsequent risks once we act and implement systems based on these research findings.

Trusting algorithms may literally kill less people today. What I am attempting to take into account is the next day, when brainpower stalls and gritty, hardworking, independent people are no longer desirable. This has been well-documented and depicted directly in Hollywood films and popular culture repeatedly.

I argue that this example (the pending swing to a self-driving world) is not inevitable, and that this is a separate issue from fossil fuels and the pursuit of green energy. I advocate for individual freedoms, but not fossil fuels. I am certainly not against change, nor do I wish to keep people locked up in hazardous working conditions. It saddens me when people confuse me for a luddite, or worse—a hater of all progress, stuck in the past.

These words here are my swing at change, my hopeful welcoming of an arrival of new thought. This world aches for humanists to rise, like they have before in waves, collaborating in order to keep inner-automation from swallowing our mindfulness. I am searching for the poets of the 21st century, the voices carrying the lineage of the enlightened, the transcendental, the beat, speaking freshly and rosy, speaking for the whole, speaking for the individual. The people are all over this country—I have met them—the ones who manifest harmony effortlessly, reciting the tunes of nature's eternal metaphors in their every expression, speaking with hope and glee to all. They speak it, live it through their smiles and daily lives, but rarely do they put it in words. Rise, poets!

Like when Emerson called for the next great age of American poetics and a young Whitman mailed him a primitive copy of *Leaves of Grass*, may my words rouse many great thoughts tomorrow, mobilizing hopeful humanists that haven't yet understood the whistling calls of the perfectly strange untamed.

For change to stick,
it seems wise to keep humans involved

will there be works
if not for my energetic perks?

will there be reason to train
my brain-body sane?

tangible schemes
for my hands
supreme?

I want to later grow proud
finally gleam

12

To Dibble,

They want a movement, but will not physically get rid of their smartphones—

It is not that they're against this all. They want to spend time away from the devices, without having to get rid of them completely. They still want the option to connect to the internet and use a phone to their advantage when things get rough (and the breaking point just keeps shrinking). I argue that this is even more dangerous of a position to take, as they think that they are above the mindlessness, above the essence of phone-abuse. Their mindset sets an example to others that smartphone ownership *can* be balanced. They watch and agree when I point out others obsessively scrolling in public, but if I don't mention it, they let it go without thinking twice about the implications when it happens again. I fear that their mindset is what got us to where we're at now, with 90+% smartphone ownership in the U.S.—

No one thinks that they have a problem with their own device use.

I've still been having a good time with everyone and haven't gotten too down about the band calling it quits, but in a way it's all relieving. Now I'm left planning the next phase of my life and you know more than anyone where my passions are. What matters is the road and the madness and riding the tidal wave of smartphone resistance and digging for truth. . .

The bus is insured, registered, seats out. Been working on it every weekend but we have it parked north of Buffalo, so progress is slow. The thing is ready to go cross-country, just need to build couches, bunks, mini-kitchen, solar? Would be nice to get a few panels to power some lights, heat for cooking?

There is plenty of verbal excitement from others, but disagreement upon a few conditions. People want some sort of all-inclusive-vacation-bus trip all while undermining the philosophy of the road, planning to outvote me on phone rules. I try not to act like an authoritarian but you know I could never go hands off with this and let them bring along 2-3 devices each, etc.

They believe that laptops are just giant phones and that all devices are practically the same. Maybe they can be convinced—they ride waves of madness and shake the grappling constraints of society, but often are the first to resort to it and cave when things get unsure. They have been inciteful in the past, but worry me with certain statements and would take some convincing to get on board for an outright smartphone pushback bus trip.

I have a few options moving forward. These decisions are important—of course they will direct my life moving forward.

13

April, 2019

It was getting warm
people were stretching their limbs in anticipation
dreaming of running free
running through the comfortable air again

The internet bill, neglected, led to an end of internet service at our house. At first it felt unnatural, although the house was built in 1893 and ran for years without electricity. Since its termination, even finer feelings of freedom left me reading more, thinking more, and noticing restored sleep.

Dibble and Brea arrived to Rochester spontaneously one day, stirred up with madness and eager to hear about where the bus was and how everything was going. They spoke of others under similar impressions that were living out in Albany and Troy.

I still was unsure about the exact policy of phones on the bus. Optimally, all riders would have already turned in their smartphones in exchange for flip phones before the trip began. This is a lot to ask for. Instead, could a "box" be implemented, acting as a drop spot for all smart devices upon entry to the bus?

Is there any purpose for an office-style setup? How far should we take it? One landline and a hot spot turns into a system more advanced than I anticipated, and in effect is no different than the levels of any other household. We need to really unplug! That's not unplugging!

In actuality
there really requires nothing but eyes and ears
hands and feet
desire for fun
diesel

no office setup
no landline
no hotspot

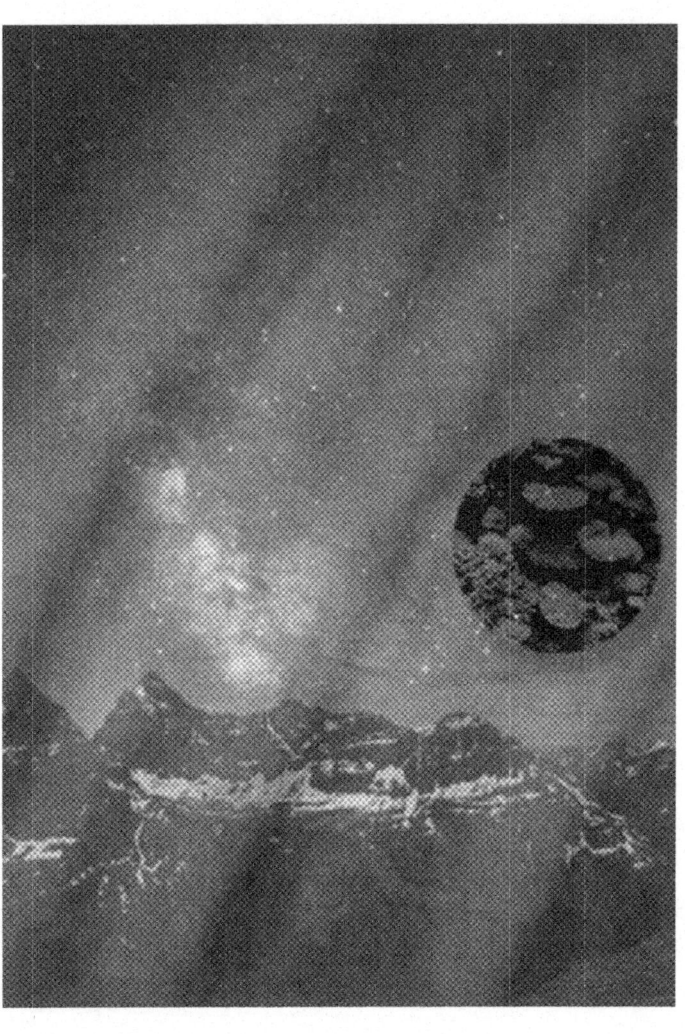

part two

BUS AS HOME

14

June, 2019
Out at Lehman Park with the bus—
Potsdam, New York

My lease was over. I needed three open credits to complete my degree. Dr. Bob knew this and created a seminar at SUNY Potsdam concentrated on Navajo and Akwesasne Mohawk cultures, linking the pressures of modernization efforts with indigenous people across American history. It would be a short summer course, situated in time between runaway trips to his ranch on the front range of South Colorado.

A lovely piano trio was playing on the radio. I made friends with the university police when an officer approached that evening to get a look at the blue bird and check for my daily parking pass. I had one, having stopped at the police station on campus before attending my first class in over two years.

It was nighttime, and after the friendly encounter I decided against leaving town to find camp and stayed around, backing into the familiar riverside at Lehman Park and staying mostly unnoticed in time to turn the loud engine off and cut my headlights.

Some time had passed since I left Rochester. Upon the conclusion of our lease, I left everything but the bus behind and briefly went West again to work with Dr. Bob. I was still riding the waves of that sweet travel groove, as all reality turns romantic and interconnected on the road in ways that thrill even the simplest moments and turn them into mystical collisions of cosmic madness just like how Kerouac and the beats dug so hard for and found in their travels.

The visions still live

It isn't that settling in one place with a stationary house can't be mystical. I never felt that way. I was just fixed on the lure of getting back on the move that was ever-refreshing, serving my roving spirit and connecting me with the simplicity of my high-spirited yearnings.

As another milestone approaches
plenty of time left to reflect
prepare for the next evolution,
allow for space to breathe—

No need to be superfluous
(say too much)
it will become
nothing at all.

Let the light catch the page
become a new form,
unlike the next page
or the last.

Where words left off
the rhythm kept up
the paper, unstamped
the music—worn in

But in the end
it is the words still standing
when the music is over
and our time has come.

Go, go,
fill that page with words
when you hear the beauty of Earth!

15

What a joy—the improvised sunroof (in place of the old emergency exit hatch) was complete, just in time for a late morning drizzle at Brown's Bridge.

I was first brought to Brown's Bridge years ago, after a long summer backpacking trip with the college. On our way back to campus, Maggs pulled the van over abruptly and we took off our sweaty boots and jumped into the fast Racquette river—after landing you have to almost immediately take off for the shore or the current will send you right down and along.

There's another spot, just a few hundred feet from the bridge upstream, where canoes can enter and catch the flow right on past the bridge and down to Potsdam—I could never forget the day that Grippe, Maggs, and I canoed from this spot to Maxfield's, one of the few bars in Potsdam, it sitting right on the Racquette and acting as a great destination after a ride along the river.

Now I'm here with the bus, after a successful interruption-free night at the lot of the canoe put-in. The sign says "open to the public without discrimination" with no reference to camping or overnight parking.

Upon arrival yesterday I jumped into the river and let the current carry me down to the bridge, running fast and even higher than usual. Despite the hot and sunny weather I had the place to myself, aside from two horses in their pen along the river, prancing around the field as I swam. They've been there much longer than I had ever known.

It was a joy, sitting outside of the bus in a folding chair with my little portable stove ripping water to a boil. I enjoyed those simple nights because they brought me back to those everlasting feelings of a drifter's life, reminding me of universal moods as they take new forms. What a different place Potsdam had become since my first semester as a student in 2013, when they couldn't control dissent and freshman ran wild. They decided to throw out Dibble before we made it to Halloween. Many others were gone before the spring came.

But over the years they didn't kick me out, long enough for me to gather memories of resting under the willow trees and sitting in the meadows. As years passed, it seemed that the people that stayed calmed down, and the crazy ones sporadically departed one at a time. Is this what it feels like to age?

I ran away to Lehman park in frigid weather once, with a borrowed book written by Victor Wooten, the day before finals week began, to sleep in the woods and find solitude. My tests that semester had nothing to do with Victor Wooten or solitude but it sure helped.

16

Resting at a lean-to
perched on a hill
listening to rock-strewn stream,
bird chirps at sundown.

Clear through the dense forest
contours of glowing mountains shine,
tempting me to climb a tree
see over the blocking leaves
peer on—

I arrived at a familiar trailhead around 4 pm, a lot semi-full, with a few scattered groups of young folks hanging around their respective cars, one group most clearly returning after at least a long weekend out in the wilderness. It was clear by their bandanas tying up their hair and bright but ragged synthetic hiking outfits. They didn't question the bus.

It was the Upper Works trailhead, in the Adirondack mountains, a quieter one for the High Peaks region but *discovered* nonetheless. I intended on making my way through Wallface the next day. Indian Pass, too, and maybe a mountain before I head back to Potsdam to continue my class with Dr. Bob.

It was Henderson Mountain and the Santanonis that sat behind the trees, opposite from the Macintyre Mountains. The latter were a bit more well known, consisting of Algonquin, Wright, and Marshall.

After a few miles of hiking down trail, I stopped and set up a beautiful bearline before dinner, pinning my orange reflective food bag between three trees on a line of paracord real taught. The sky was turning pink, a little orange, although I couldn't make out any definitive edges of color because of the massive clouds across the sky.

The stream continues to flow
run on fast water!
From the mountains to the villages
and back again;
fast may you run.

Under the brightness of the morning sky, I followed blue, red, yellow trailhead markers and trekking pole scratches in rock, wandering through Indian Pass and around beautiful Wallface to the mighty Lake Colden.

Heavy pack, books, wool blanket, tent, lots of food—not great footwear which seemed okay until about mile 10 or so. There was not much human activity on trail, although the paths were beaten down and muddy from the weekend before.

The trails were difficult to navigate at times— unexplored territory of my own eyes up to Colden, which was true relief and grace upon feet as the trails opened up and the dam awaited with its wooden bridge and view of mountains all around.

Mount Colden stared down at me, reminding me of my birthday hike with Jeremy in true tough weather, slopes slick and icy to our lack of spikes.

We persisted from trail marker to trail marker until the terrain turned to all rock and no tree. Usually it was okay as the rocks were marked with yellow paint in the direction of travel, but soon the snow covered too much rock and upon a handful of risky advances and doubtful lunges we lost the trail and finally turned around instead of hiking up and over.

That's Colden, and since then I had not been back. I chatted with two fellas headed up there on my third morning—I was tempted to hop along but I had five and a half miles to cover to the trailhead already and ached from the long day before.

Upon return to the head of the trail, I found the bus unharmed, with no note or ticket like back in the Tetons. FM signal was nonexistent but CB picked up a regional weather forecast and recap.

I arrived to Potsdam around 9:30 pm, pulling into Dr. Bob's driveway with the bus to prepare for a day of work on his house the next morning.

17

Pen-on-paper,
beautifully impermanent!
hold it for a day
watch me pull away—
don't believe that the chance was lost

Opposite parallels
immediate magic
little talk
but autumn?

I could feel it
the excitement,
the unpredictable
Grasping weakly to the enduring mystic

Long travel
lost in bookstores, long
find the rocky coast

future—
the present too pleasant
could write a million words to explain
but it's clear now

18

To relinquish a search
full of unchecked desire,
I dispelled mental distractions
turning strength into harmony

No worth ruminating over definitives;
true closure is a myth

Too frequently I'm found caught up
treading in limbo over regular decisions.
I wondered how this story would turn out

happy or tragic

Opportunity surrounds the enchanted,
                                    infinite

but our lives are not
What will show tonight?

Please take care
refine your stare
hold back, nightmare
Can we be fair?

I wonder if art is eternal
or will pass with all else
aside from the voice of the now
just waiting to speak

blues,
                    violets,

today's
                    roots.

But to move too fast
or to move too slow—
To out-pursue
or to be left a lonely low?

If this was the end
how it had to be
I wouldn't shed another, me.
I too will fade again.

I wonder at Moon's rays—
do they still burn bright
those fiery cool eyes?

Has the dust yet settled?
Could it be
that once is bright can dim
fast and thin?

19

August, 2019
Troy, New York

Dibble and I hit the road abruptly again, this time after receiving word that a good friend of his living in Denver had lost a partner. We considering hitchhiking out for a moment but elected to take the bus as it was the most reliable and practical mode of travel within reach. We took the most direct path we could—a straight hustle to Denver—avoiding thruways once we passed Cleveland, slowing us down but creating a straighter line on the map. The decision quickly filled our trip with sporadic run-ins with locals rather than travelers passing by thruway truck stops. A mix of both was best. We barely had the money and in fact had all but ran out several miles before reaching Denver—rationing did no use as the bus ate up hundreds of dollars each day in fuel as we propelled west.

It was able to work because we both had the available time and guts. He lined it up with his current employer to take the time off and I was available, having just completed my degree and with no absolute plan or pull. I was looking for something new. Dibble's spirit was as wild and true as ever, so tuned in with the present moment that it didn't matter what happened as long as we reached Chico and could spend a bit of valuable time with him. He had been offered a few new jobs within that last month, and stood on the brink of leaving his current situation just briefly or using the gap to start something entirely new.

I was not as close with Chico as he was, but I was more than willing to offer my support. The bus had little purpose in the northeast by then, as did myself. I was excited to be presented with another chance to go west, especially this one being with my original road pal.

We still dreamt and conversed of what it would take to kick off a movement, keeping in touch over the years after we returned to New York phoneless in 2014. He had found a community in Troy that quenched his madness, and a companion that meshed with him wonderfully. He wasn't entirely content with his job at the time, but they treated him well and offered him pay for the time he requested off to go west. He told them he only needed a week and received it pliably.

20

The sun was setting somewhere around Peoria, Indiana as we pulled up to a lively gas station that naturally seemed like the center of town. It was tight so I elected against pulling up to a pump and instead parked on the front edge of the property near the intersection. Dibble was snoozing, preparing for his next shift at the wheel, when I returned through the front doors of the bus to wake him. A curious duo of raggedy young street kids on bikes followed me into the gas station as I pulled in, approaching me immediately and wondering what a bus of such sorts was doing rolling through their town. They couldn't have been sixteen but each had small unlit cigarette stubs in their hands and one of them kept talking about how I needed to watch the other do a wheelie.

Dibble stumbled out of the bus a few moments later, unknowing of our location or the time of day, holding a hazy impression that it was the morning sun rising and that he had slept through the night. "What time is it?" Dibble asked the three of us who had already been chatting for a moment.

When one of them told Dibble that it was about seven, he continued to believe that it was morning. He realized that the strange kids were getting kicks of this, and instead of looking for further clarification took the act further and exaggerated his expressions to their amusement, dropping his sagging pants to the ground and drawing them up quickly before cracking a bad-mannered joke that of course they erupted at and only drew their ears closer.

We told them we needed money for fuel in order to continue on, and that we needed to get to work. Time to mingle! In no time Dibble found an opportunity as an old man pulled up no more than twenty feet from the front of the bus and needed help changing a tire. Right on it! The adolescents tried to help and did unscrew a few bolts but when the man handed Dibble a twenty-dollar bill and they asked for a share, he said, "you kidding me, this is America, kids."

Immediately we put the money in the tank and fired up the engine, sending them the notion that it was time we get moving. "But wait," they pleaded, "can we have a ride up the hill?" One of their bikes was barely operative, even though the other *could* do a serious wheelie.

Of course, we agreed and loaded their bikes into the bus through the back door. I drove and Dibble sat back with the two kids under the red interior lights that go on automatically with the headlights. "Just one catch. Those things aren't allowed," I heard Dibble say as he pointed at their bright smartphones in hand.

I looked back for a moment and studied their matching expressions. They looked uncomfortable, worried that we were ready to kidnap them or something, but they listened and complied with the request to keep their phones away. I thought back to the box idea that was initially proposed. Would they have noticed it if it was labeled? Would it have been easier for them to not only comply but *understand* before they boarded? How could it be made clearer?

"So you guys don't have phones?"

"What do you mean, we have CB radio!"

When we arrived at the next gas station and parked at a diesel pump, the kids began to multiply.

More of their friends were already there, some looking even younger, but all of them were dying to climb on. Dibble led them up to the roof and soon there were too many to count. Others at the gas station were beginning to believe that we *knew* these people. Yes, maybe we did, but we only met them thirty minutes ago!

In the midst of the fiasco, a few guys about our age or maybe a few years older offered Dibble a handful of tomatoes from their farm up the road. The kids were running wild, but once the older gentleman realized that we didn't know any of them he made them scram.

"Get lost, little kids! Let these guys go!"

He wanted us to head to their place and dock for the night, but Dibble and I knew we needed to shake everyone while we could and get on out of town.

After the split, Dibble and I began recalling the event. "Their faces were priceless when you dropped the bomb on their phones."

But there was something missing. There was something empty about having to *tell* them to put them away. It's easy to relate to the frustrations of running around with too much shapeless effort, trying to tell people things that they did not wish to hear, showing them things they just don't want to see.

Dibble knew this, and reiterated that the only thing to do is embody the desires we hope others will grasp. There is no use talking about it or bringing it up. The idea is the example of your phoneless life, a display of life under the impression that smartphones did not even matter and were not worth it.

We were just a few wandering bus-dwellers from the east, but our embodiments had surely made their evening.

21

Country roads
space

hours to gaze over the time

Somewhere along the trafficless open road, a wild-looking beast dog gazed at the bus as we raced by it. We had no choice but to pull over and turn back. It was even bigger looking when it caught sight of the bus and approached to check us out. Dibble tried to throw it some bait but the beast had just the right idea: to flee back into the high cornfields confidently, knowing his outer limits, where he was, and how far to go.

There were minor setbacks. The bus needed a break and refused to start without a jump somewhere in the land of nowhere. We also hit a surreal, epilepsy-imposing lightning storm in Kansas that explained why the famous Wizard of Oz was set there. Petty bickering surfaced between us as I worried over his attention to the road when he drove and I looked over his shoulder. All in all, it only took a small helping of transmission fluid and three days of endless diesel filling to make it to Kirk, Colorado.

Kirk was still a Kansas-esque town—out of sight were the mountain views and nonexistent was the liveliness. There was nothing yet welcoming us like we hoped Colorado would.

Early in the morning, very low on gas, we raced down from Kirk to the interstate junction that ran to

Denver. With little effort from us the bus was revered at our first stop—people wanted to help support our crusade. I had an old blue 5-gallon fuel tank in the bus that, upon carrying it out of the bus for a few moments, was quickly filled up with diesel. There was only one problem that we failed to realize until it was already full: the spout was broken and would not cleanly send the fuel into the tank.

What was an alternative? We thought quickly. Looking around we noticed a large orange traffic cone serving no purpose and sporadically decided that it was a good idea to promptly funnel the fuel through the cone into the tank of the bus. Did it work? Some of it made it into the tank, but most of it soaked the cone and landed on the ground. Soon a manager caught sight of the act and approached. Thankfully, he was kind and brought out a hose to pour the fuel through cleanly.

"I could get you into some real trouble if I turn you in for helping us with this risky business and something goes wrong," Dibble said to the manager. "Nobody light a match here."

The young manager was in a good mood.

"Actually, diesel doesn't ignite like average gasoline. You couldn't start a fire with this if you tried. Diesel ignites on pressure."

"So that's why truckers smoke at the pumps."

Lots of funny looks from that manager.

22

By then we were just one last push away from the massive Denver International Airport. We headed straight for it upon Chico's suggestion, avoiding the map's green toll road at all costs. We were unsure of Denver's parking accessibility for something like the bus, and decided upon docking it and taking on the city by foot before marching in with the 35-footer. After the long drive it felt great to step away from the wheel and walk lightly under the big sky.

We found ourselves not quite at the airport but at a nearby rail stop pointing west with a massive lot almost full but with no other school buses to blend in with. The pay-system was odd—after finding the machine and feeding it four dollars, the receipt read, "do not place on dash" and displayed our license plate number, leading us to wonder who was checking the lot.

"Cameras, perhaps?" Soon we realized they had every inch of the lot covered with cameras. "They're really just throwing jobs away, if nothing else."

Quickly we hopped on the rail, a spotless one that must had just been built, and followed the blue line to downtown.

People often asked how we got around without a GPS. It was actually rather fun, and locals were always around to help out if (when) you miss something. That being said, roads undoubtedly have their unpredictable stretches. I figured it had always been that way, but perhaps it had gotten worse—split roads in the same town under the same name, confusing turns *meant* to throw off those not in the know, and the list goes on. As more and more choose the GPS to assist them, perhaps it explained why the common citizen so often struggled to explain directions to others that they had driven down before hundreds of times. That was often our biggest obstacle.

"You made it all of the way across the country without a GPS?" It was easier when travelling big distances to follow a map. But when city roads tighten and finding the destination comes down to dialing in on a specific address, paper maps became more difficult to follow and a stronger grasp on the area was needed to keep up.

When we finally linked up with Chico it was a big relief. Through only phone calls and texts, it can be difficult to understand the actuality of such a situation—it became essentially our duty to reach him in person, to receive the closure, and to be left with the peace of mind. We didn't want to act like we had driven all this way just to see him—we were doing it for ourselves and the sake of travel too—but seeing him was surely the destination. It was a priority for Dibble and soon me too to let him know that two old New York hooligans were there for him.

23

Our initial linkup with Chico was brief as he had a work shift to attend to that evening, so Dibble and I went back off on our own to make something of the remainder of leftover day. Chico's friend joined us on our brief walk back to the train station, where the three of us sat for a moment to lock down a plan before he diverged. I wanted to make our way over to Boulder while Chico was at work, but we were unsure of whether to take public transportation to get there or to backtrack to the bus and get there with our own set of rolling wheels.

A strange man sitting across from us at the station with that unmistakable look of a high-spirited passerby in his eye provided us with a few words of advice as we readied to make our decision. "Take the big blue bus to Boulder. You will meet amazing, famous people there."

Of course, he knew nothing of our bus back at the airport. Whether or not there was a public bus heading to Boulder, his words were enough for me to insist on returning to the blue one marked 95.

The bus was safe and sound when we returned to it. To Boulder we drove as the night rose over the mountain contours and day turned to dusk. I wanted to find Naropa University, a tiny school in Boulder that was founded in 1974 by Allen Ginsberg, Anne Waldman, Gary Snyder, and many others, all heroes of mine. Dibble knew how much I wanted to find the place and agreed to make it our next brief destination.

The night had fallen by the time we reached Boulder, but I knew the school was on Arapahoe Avenue and eventually we found Naropa's main campus. There was no chance of parking onsite with the bus, but just next door there was a children's center with an empty lot that worked fantastically. We had no grasping idea pertaining to the limits of the campus, where it ended, or whether the enormous building across the river past the Naropa sign was associated or something else. We followed a bike path that split the residence halls with a few other small buildings, walking right past the border of Naropa and over to the castle-looking structure in the distance. It was conveniently the first weekend of the fall semester, so we had no difficulty fitting in as aimless young wanderers.

"Where's the dining hall?" Dibble asked a pair of students walking from the castle. They looked at us funny but pointed further down the way. We walked a little further but soon decided it was a lost cause.

"So, is this your place? Do you feel the energy you've been looking for?"

I felt good but I wasn't yet satisfied. The castle-building was the University of Colorado, a whole different beast. We elected to take a different path back to the bus in my hopes of finding something more definitively Naropa. On the road across from the residence halls, we followed a path to a small courtyard with a handful of tables and chairs, surrounded by a few more small buildings. One had an enormous, beautifully decorated ancient swing outside of its door that looked like it belonged in a museum. Drawn to it, we learned that we were at the doors of the Allen Ginsberg library.

There was an engraved William Blake quote on the wall of the library. The two of us read this over and over again before quarreling over its meaning. It resonated in the air around us, reminding me of the trends of all life, although Dibble did not initially take a liking for it.

"He who binds to himself a joy
Does the winged life destroy;
But he who kisses the joy as it flies
Lives in eternity's sun rise."

"Isn't it a good thing to be bound to joy? How would that destroy?"

I thought long and hard before choosing my words. I recited a line from a familiar translation of the Tao Te Ching: "*Those who are bound by desire see only the outward container.*"

"I agree with that," Dibble responded. "It's no good to be bound to desire. But bound to joy? I see that as desirable."

I thought of the many forms of smothered obsession, *bound to joy*, the unpleasant expressions of affection that repel sweet connection.

Maybe we have heard this before. But I agreed with Dibble too, as to approach joy and love with laziness can so easily strain.

After writing down the Blake quote on a scrap piece of paper and filing it away in my wallet, I felt satisfied, despite the campus being empty and too dark to gather a sensory opinion of. *But something was there*, and our short debate over the poem left me with an impression of the school that struck my aspiration to return.

I felt that the bus was not safe for much longer in its position at the children's center, and after speaking with a pedestrian we decided not to walk any closer towards the action of Pearl Street.

"Brandon's living up in Fort Collins," I said. "I tried to link up with him last time I passed through but it didn't work out. Have you heard from him?"

And in just a few fast moments, like so many of our decisions, our next destination became the residence of another old friend.

24

Darkness blanketed the sky for the whole drive up to Fort Collins, but the route on the map appeared like one simple and straight connection out of Boulder. I tried a backroad shortcut and soon had to backtrack, but soon we were passing Loveland and narrowing in on our destination.

The easy way turned confusing once we started looking for Elizabeth street. Brandon's instructions were to take Elizabeth just about to the end, and that we would find his domain just before the foothills of the mountains. Little did we know that there were two Elizabeth streets in Fort Collins, so we ended up wasting a whole bunch of time driving slowly past each intersection on the wrong Elizabeth looking for his turn, finding no foothills.

After a few laps, which required a whole lot of effort when a simple three-point turn was no quick maneuver, we found Brandon standing out in the street waving us in. We found a quick street side lacking a no parking sign just a few blocks away from his house, and there locked up the bus for the night.

Lots of laughs and stories to exchange—

We smelled. He had us both take showers before anything else. It was great to see Brandon prospering in Colorado, especially because of all the talks we had in high school about going west and starting new lives.

The very next day, the three of us plus Argie, a friend of Brandon's also from New York, made the hilarious decision of driving through Estes Park and into the heart of Rocky Mountain National Park. It was a real scare for the riders of the bus as we steered up and around sharp corners with nothing in sight off the sharp edges of the cliffsides.

At a scenic pull-off on the edge of freedom and death we finally pulled over and decided it would be the furthest we would reach. We brought lawn chairs up to the roof of the bus and had a righteous time sitting on top of the planet, studying the alpine sights, looking many miles into the distance. I prayed for the sake of the brakes—if they were to go at that point, there would be nothing to do but get out of the way because everything would have been history.

On the way down I searched for a place to have my national parks passport stamped, but the place was closed so I settled on a souvenir magnet at the visitor center. Brandon was in a hurry to get back for a fantasy football draft so we hustled back. He wanted us to stay the night so we could go out on the water the next day, but Dibble was looking to get back to Chico—we had already spent too much time on our excursion without including him.

The moments in Fort Collins would be treasured but we had to get back on the road again, following a new address given to Dibble from Chico in Lakewood. Of course, that drive took a bit longer than expected, but before frustration could build too high, we met a resourceful character who went by Leaf at a corner side gas station when we stopped to fuel up and regather our sense of direction.

They were pushing the homeless out of Denver, even more so in Boulder, driving up rent and pushing the squatters out of their old havens. This was old news, but the people were not yet gone.

When I walked by Leaf to give the clerk the last few dollars we had to fuel up, he asked me how I was doing. "Broke, my friend."

Before we left, he trotted up to the small driver's side window of the bus and handed me three quarters. Most would expect a man of his appearance and demeanor to be asking for the money, but instead he was giving what he had. It didn't take long before we invited him into the bus to have a brief chat. The local insight he gave us regarding Lakewood was quality, and directed us right where we needed to head next. Thanks, Leaf!

25

Rolled in under perfect circumstances—
Bus matching the length of the driveway
greeted happily
new friends to meet

Gathering for the sake of art,
—paint gathering—
show them off
let the crafts be admired as they unfold

I sat on the ground for most of the time
watching and perceiving,
recuperating after a long push
thinking of the next move

Brooklyn was the host. She had an array of wild
paintings sitting on her mantle, and even wilder stories
for each one. She cooked us all pasta with a spicy sauce
and later brewed everyone a big pot of hot tea.

I would have loved for either of them to paint
something on or in the bus. I loved the Partridge Family
look it had going, but it needed more hand-painted
touches. Ryan had a few connections with local Denver
muralist friends, and recommended them after really
thinking over the task. He knew it would take some
madness for someone to pull off a school bus mural-
job.

Ryan gave us a stack of stickers that he
designed. He was working on a really impressive

painting that night, a symmetrical piece with passionate colors and meticulous detail.

After a wonderful gathering and tour of the bus, the 5 of us divided, us taking Chico with us back to Denver. On the way back, we spoke of taking a trip of our own to the mountains, especially if Chico could free himself from work for a short time.

We stayed the night at his place in the Five Points neighborhood of urban Denver. I wishfully hoped for the ambitious bus-painter to reach out to us, but instead the three of us marked up the bus the next day using what I had for spray paints and a few tubes of assorted acrylic colors.

Chico took us on a deep walk to the center of the city, all the way past Colfax Avenue, through the massive public library, and up to a nearby art museum. What an eclectic city! Even several of the homeless felt approachable and friendly, happy to be in Denver.

After a return to Five Points, amidst talk about the near future, Dibble decided to look into the going rates for airfare back to New York. By then it was clear that driving back with the bus was not an option. I was intending on staying west indefinitely, faced with a complete lack of funds, along with stronger connections and aspirations in Colorado than New York. I needed to stay and he needed to leave.

A fly-cheap website revealed that there was no time to wait, and that he was to take the ticket out for the very next day in order to save a large bundle of money. The plan to hit the country was complete, the slim chance of us traveling further on, history—quickly changing my mindset but not completely unexpectedly by then. Dibble was facing a tough decision back east, as the week of grace was nearing complete with his current job. Because of the treatment he was given from them, he changed his mind in regards to leaving them for good, and decided to take the chance to fly home and return the very next day.

26

And very early the next morning we left metropolitan Denver and headed back for the airport with the bus. In just a blink he was off, *just like that.*

It was sad to see him off but highly anticipated was my next step. He loaned me $40 dollars to float on, which felt like a sturdy security blanket at the time. For the next three days I drifted between Boulder and Nederland, fixated on Naropa and the Flat Iron mountains that stared down at the city.

Naropa was my immediate destination after putting the bus in drive and pulling out from the airport. The children's center parking lot was a no-go—filled—so I settled on the grocery store parking lot just a few blocks up Arapahoe, knowing my time would be limited to an hour or so there. Before departing, I drew up a simple note to tape to the bus door: "Visiting Naropa University today. Please do not tow. Thank you!"

O to walk another campus
in attempt to pass as student,
pacing down Arapahoe
right back to the courtyard that I remembered
from a street-lit-night-visit from before

The library was open, so I walked in and sat down after pulling a book from a shelf. I didn't stay long, but admired the tranquility of the place—fairly full of students but tremendously quiet.

Shelves loaded with eye-catchers.

After departing, I turned to the building next door that which dictated admissions. The elderly receptionist inside was a sweetheart. After introducing myself as a prospective graduate student, she handed me a number of pamphlets of various sizes and wrote a phone number and email on a yellow sticky-note. She provided me with my first direction, my first connection to faculty. All aside, perhaps the most important thing she gave me was a pocket size map that folded out elaborately to detail Naropa's three campuses.

From there I left and drove right to the Nalanda campus, also on Arapahoe but uptown many blocks, resting along the train tracks and amongst a field of prairie dog burrows. At the corner was a sheltered bus stop, and to the west a beautiful view of the Flat Irons and the canyon past the city.

Nalanda
different
campus of the writing department
bus fits in the parking lot.

It was even quieter than the prior campus I came from, and much more open. The sky seemed bigger. The prior was tight-knit and welcoming, but this one vaster in its wide-ranging appeal, more rugged in its aura.

After tacking my note back on the bus, I trotted inside to take a few laps around the one-building-campus. Interesting artwork and event posters from Naropa's beginnings filled the walls. I smiled at a few variously-aged strangers. Each face shined back with positive regard.

Again brief, I headed back to the bus feeling inspired but introspectively. After sitting back in the driver's seat and preparing to start the bus, a few fast moments passed before a figure walked up to my open doors and tapped on the glass. She had her hair tied up with a bandana, and dark blue overalls reaching her feet.

"I must admit, you drew my curiosity—I take it you're a new student? Love your bus!"

I admitted that I was not enrolled, and just a wandering traveler. She said the bus was very "Naropa-esque" and was eager to chat, even more-so after learning that I was just passing through.

"I'm sitting out by the tracks having lunch if you'd like to join. Check this out, there's a whole stack out there if you're interested—"

It was a bundle of old railroad ties. My mother always told me to grab as many as I could if I ever got the chance. "They won't be around long on my watch!"

I accepted her offer for lunch and enjoyed her company, as she became my first Naropa friend and window into their way of life. It was her last semester as a student in the art therapy program, so she had plenty of things to say about the school, and places to recommend I search for around town.

She told stories of hitchhiking in her youth, homeless and transient, riding freight trains across thousands of American miles, and finally settling in Boulder just a few years ago. Her stories revealed her age, but her demeanor reflected her persisting liveliness.

She explained the public bus system, free for students and six dollars for the public. There were all sorts of lines accessible with a day pass, including lines to Nederland and Denver, along with all around Boulder. I wanted to find Pearl Street. I had already packed a bag to take for the day with my juggling balls and other short-term necessities like water, snacks, and layers.

"You think they'll mind if I leave the bus here for a few hours?"

"You'll be fine."

The lot was quiet, just a handful of cars parked, and I felt confident with my note, so my new friend and I left the tracks and headed up to the bus stop. While we were waiting, there was another girl already at the stop that she knew. I was getting the positive impression that the community was a tight-knit one.

Wheeling down Arapahoe now
seated on a fantastic community bus

Let me off at Pearl,
red brick pass
where the cars are forbidden,
and the eclectic try their talents
for pennies and a glance.

27

I had my juggling balls,
but I wouldn't pull them out
if there were other jugglers on the block

they were always better than me
and I preferred to watch
observe
give the talented the stage.

One day I did ask a pedal steel player
sitting on a Corner
if he minded me posting up
throwing to his hums and strums.
—no problem!—

I always juggled better with a rhythm
something for viewers to lock in with
follow as they pass

After standing out a fair distance away from the
musician and juggling out on my own for about a half
hour, I stopped and approached him.

"Any luck out there?" he asked politely.

"Just a few donations, but I owe it to you, that
thing sounds fantastic. It's still really clear, even from a
distance."

"There's a good reason they call these things
resonators, no joke my friend—"

It was getting dark. I was up seven dollars on the day, just enough to cover the cost of the bus pass. I enjoyed the people of the streets and mingled with many of them but by then I was ready to find the mountains.

West past the limits of development
Canyon road—Boulder creek,
where fallen rocks
tumble down the vertical
threatening the paved pathways
leading to Nederland

Upon arrival
I see a sign in a window:
Maps, Tourist Information
I pop the question,
"know where I could park a bus?"

The seated bearded man knew well
sending me north
high country
nobody-land
(rainbow lakes)
plenty of room for the bus.

28

Between a safe-spot in the desolate high-country north of Nederland by night and the lively Pearl street mall by day, I commuted between the distinctive landscapes, each with their own charming scenes and views to offer.

Hitchhikers accompanied me more often than not on this route, it being so practical and popular, acting as one of the only paths out of Boulder and directly into the mountains. One morning, I caught sight of a tired-looking man in his 60's sitting at the bus stop in Nederland. With only a few moments to judge him, I stopped quickly and swung open the air-powered main doors like a traditional bus-driver would to pick up a cluster of students.

"Heading to Boulder?" I shouted over the engine.

"As a matter of fact, I am," the man returned as he stood up and tossed his backpack over his shoulder. He could tell I was no public bus but decided to trust my mysterious multi-colored machine passing through. I appreciated his company, and he even gave me a twenty-dollar bill in exchange for the ride after we arrived to Boulder.

Another time I was on my way back to my overnight spot past Nederland when a shaggy young man appeared on the side of the road with a thumb up and two big backpacks laying on the ground next to him. He was nowhere near the edge of town, in fact he was far from it, and looked like he had been hiking all morning.

When I stopped to ask him if he needed a ride, he declined and explained that he was waiting for his friend to return from a run to town. He would have liked to accept my ride, but didn't want to ditch his friend's luggage and drift away from their reunion point. I told him not to worry and that perhaps I would give him a ride if I saw him again. Paul was his name.

I thought it was the last time we would meet.

A few hours after I arrived at my spot, took a nap, and cooked dinner, I received a startling, mysterious knock on the bus doors. I was many miles not only from town but from where I last saw Paul, and had not seen or heard any other cars pull up to the area after I did.

Paul was a very soft-spoken, phoneless wanderer, but frankly his friend Ron was neither one of those. They had hiked at least 10 miles with serious elevation change to reach me and the bus, which surprised me but was nonetheless very impressive. They had no real plan but to drift and see the country, and told me wild stories of sleeping in the woods with no tent and making small cooking fires in strict fire-ban country. Ron's overpacked backpack rig was hilarious—clearly a novice like so many other new drifters that so frequently overpack but soon realize that half of what they brought is absolutely not worth the weight upon their shoulders.

"So where are *you* headed?" they asked me, the mysterious bus driver. I told them the Denver area for a three-day run of Phish shows in Commerce City starting the very next night.

At that point, I had barely any money left from juggling. Dibble's donation was dwindling. The show was sold-out and I had no tickets, but I wanted to go for a chance to hear the music and undertake a change of pace in my life. I loved the band, but there was also something special about meeting the fascinating people that showed up and formed the scene around each show. Not knowing whether or not the music could be heard from outside of the gates, I headed there anyways, taking the vagabonds along.

Transients aplenty
traveling, arriving from afar
creating temporary community
one by one

29

Outstanding a setback
to detach from recall,
astounded by my present,
unwilling to look back,
even in pouring rain

After spending three evenings in Commerce City, I was left with just enough money for a confident shot at another change of setting. Between night one and two of the three-day run, I dropped Ron off at the local Greyhound station pointing to his midwestern hometown of Kansas City, although Paul stuck around with me for all three nights of music.

We were successful at selling bottles of water and cans of Rolling Rock outside of the show, along with utilizing the bus to shuttle fans from the parking lot to the hotels afterward, all while turning plenty of strangers into friends. Having to pay for three parking spaces each night proved worthy in exchange for wide-ranging encounters aplenty, along with tips both tangible and implied, tips that would have otherwise been sent off to gloomy taxi drivers and flashy party limos.

Following the second show, Paul and I fired up the bus after selling out of water and the crowd had started to die down. Just a few moments before takeoff, I was left in the driver's seat unable to speak in the middle of a mouthwash rinse when five mysterious women presented themselves in front of the headlights of the bus to lift up their shirts and reveal their bare chests in an effort to grab my attention. I could not believe my eyes, and tried to call out for Paul but could not as I resisted spitting out the window and startling the strangers who continued flashing me and cheering. Finally, I found a cup to spit into before shouting and laughing.

"We're looking for the party bus! Take us to the Double Tree!"

Surprised to find that it was just Paul and me inside, they continued with their unpredictable antics and all-around animated thrills as we departed for their hotel. Not only did they keep their breasts exposed throughout the drive, but they were having a blast as they waved to passing cars and shouted for folks at red lights to peer on as they pressed themselves against the glass of the bus windows. At that point, all I wanted was to let Paul drive because he was completely speechless and adding to the unusual circumstances in his inability to cater to the multiple women-gone-mad. He was rarely one of many words, but never was I in such dire need for a wing-man to keep things cool as we continued to their destination.

When we arrived at their hotel, a few cars had assumedly caught on to our situation and trailed us in hopes of meeting these women. All I could do was shrug my shoulders at them. The parking lot appeared full to the brim, but one of the ladies insisted I continue around to the back of the hotel. The bus was already nearly impossible for strangers to look past, but with expressive, colorful women inside it was gathering more attention than ever. I pulled around to the back of the hotel where crowds of Phish fans stood under a party tent, sat in the grass, and huddled around a few dispersed nitrous tanks around the parking lot. Immediately, their attention was turned to the loud engine rolling along. Luckily there were a few spots open in the back corner of the lot where I could slide in and park for the night.

The ladies were ever thankful to have arrived safely and in such an eclectic fashion, and invited the two of us to their hotel afterward. I couldn't believe it, as neither of us had showered any time recently and it was obvious. I noticed that my feet and ankles were visibly dirty when we arrived and I removed my sandals, and Paul's messy hair and unkept, high-cheeked beard gave away his current state of homelessness.

They gave us shoulder massages and were clearly getting excited. They were all at least in their late thirties, but were striking and charming in their forward notions and decisiveness. It was then that I made the awful mistake of retreating to their bathroom to quickly defecate. I thought that I could get away with it, but there was no fan or window in the bathroom and no hope for us from then on. I ran out to the bus and returned quickly with my pleasantly-scented lemongrass spray, gifting it to them in an attempt to make amends. They were delighted by it and accepted it as a gift from me, but the thrill was gone and after many laughs over it, they elected to disperse back into the after-party crowd behind the hotel. They found us again after night three, dressed nicely again and eager to reveal their breasts, but even though they didn't mention it, I couldn't get the prior night out of my head and in embarrassment could not look at them the same again.

When the morning arrived after the last show, I boiled water for oatmeal and coffee at a bench behind the hotel. I reminded Paul that this was the end of the road, and that we would have to split ways. He didn't have a plan moving forward other than to return to the mountains, so I decided for him and dropped him off at the western edge of Idaho Springs, Colorado.

It was there that I immediately turned south. Pushing at full speed up and over the continental divide, I was glad to be independent and transitory again. It was a new month—September—and like so frequently at beginnings of new months, a freshness came along with it that I acknowledged and enjoyed.

I picked up a lone hitchhiker in Breckenridge and took her to the next town south, conversing over the local culture until time came to split ways. She mentioned Santa Fe, talking up their artsy community and attractive grassroots scene that appeared to be inviting me as I approached it. New Mexico borders Colorado to the south, and in so always enticed me over the years. Until then I had never done more than pass through the north-eastern corner, Raton Pass, on the way to northern Texas in 2015, and Oklahoma in beautiful late May, 2019.

Still several miles to the state line,
dusk approaches.
Sign says forest service road, Poncha Springs
(forest service:
        open invitation to respectful rubber tramps)

Lucky chance to rest a night
uphill path, unpaved from start
spacious and airy
overlooking impressions of peace
visions only found in the West

Mountains, valleys, tall golden meadows
all directions, many miles, wildness,
stretching endlessly,
no sliver of cell reception.

30

Along Buena Vista and right on through the region of the Great Sand Dunes, the next skies of the day were sunlit and clear. I stopped, entered the park, and hiked around the massive, beautiful sandbanks instead of just passing them by, but sadly the touristy bothers overpowered and distracted me. Upon arrival, I climbed out of the bus and right onto the bright dunes, my bare feet digging in with each step before soon becoming too hot to resist returning to my sandals.

Mini desert enclosed by mountains
as I ascend a sand peak,
I see—
only isolated groups of walkers.
No solitary wanderers,
no big-eyed outsiders,
just me.

No such thing as a detour
today

Still south I continued when I picked up yet another hitchhiker, this one heading all the way to Santa Fe.
Just the travel guide I needed.
He wondered if I was looking for work, and explained that there was plenty of it in Ojos Caliente, a small town with a popular hot spring resort north of Santa Fe. The rest of the drive through Colorado was a

beauteous, swift coast through mostly secluded but fast country roads leading to the state line.

Across it, the roads continued through ongoing rocky-peaked mountains, carrying us through more big skied remoteness until we finally emerged at a questionable fork in the road. Road repairs in progress deterred us from the path to Ojos Caliente and Santa Fe. It appeared that we had no choice but to head for Taos, which appeared considerably out of the way upon a glance at my map. The hitchhiker expressed no remorse for the roadblock, and spoke of Taos approvingly. He informed me that I could drop him off once we reached Taos, and that the detour would surely be worth my time as a sight-seer. As a drifter of my own sort, he reiterated that I would find plenty of like-mindedness in Taos, if not more than what was waiting in Santa Fe.

Quickly, the architecture of Taos struck me. Every building within its limits seemed to be constructed of red clay, including the gas stations, grocery stores, and popular worldwide chains. It really wasn't a large city, and there seemed to be only a few major intersections of any significance, although foot-traffic and automobile congestion made up the rest of my first impression. The hitchhiker and I had lunch at a Mexican restaurant, also built of stucco and impressing me with the flavor and richness of their green chile.

The two of us parted ways after lunch. He suggested I find my way to the plaza, a popular, historic attraction. To cater to my unease regarding the tight streets and large bus we arrived in, he also explained that my best bet for overnight parking would be on the eastern outskirts of town.

"You're not the only one, the others have just already found their place to land, hide, and operate off-the-grid." Aside from the strange eco-conscious houses he regarded as "earthships" that we passed by on the outskirts of Taos, he also pointed out mysterious, anarchical mesas sitting along the furthest edge of sight. Essentially lawless, the mesas have developed into a hub of enduring desperados, acting as a retreat from modern norms and traditional law enforcement. Most locals would not dare wander up to the mesas, and doctors and medical professionals in Taos were supposedly known to ignore pleas of distress if one admitted to willingly living on the mesa. Cases were simply thrown out that had anything to do with the surreptitious land.

"Just talk around with locals—you're bound to meet someone from the mesa, whether they're stopping in town to stock up or better yet to offer up a barter with you. You'll probably find that most of them don't care much for money."

31

Let the sun shine in
right through the blinds

go dine with your friends
don't worry about the ends

Shine on, ray!

And so I wandered about, reaching the Taos plaza,
reading a few historical signposts, and even stopping to
juggle for a few moments. That being said, I wasn't
confident with my parking spot and aspired to follow
the hitchhiker's advice regarding camping. In under an
hour, I had had enough and elected to head for the
eastern outskirts as I could sense evening catching up
to me. Dodging Taos Pueblo and continuing past the
edge of the red stucco settlements, I entered the
heavily wooded Kit Carson National Forest. When the
time felt right, I stopped and parked at a small pull-off
with foothills stretching up to mountain peaks on both
sides of the road. At the edge of the shoulder was a
driveway leading down to a gorgeous ranch in the
valley ahead, but the space seemed discrete enough to
justify parking along it for the night as dusk
camouflaged the bus.

I was dangerously low on funds and fuel. When the
next morning came, I was left unsure of whether to
return to Taos or continue on to Angel Fire. I had

passed not one spacious service station in Taos, and assumed I must had been at least halfway to the next town.

What would you do? I kept Taos in the fresh, front of my mind, but continued on.

I had enough fuel to make it out of the forest and to the clearing named Angel Fire. It was a true one-blinking-traffic-light kind of town, much quieter than Taos. It presented itself with plenty of scenic views, possessing just as much appeal as I approached it.

The rest of the money I had at the time would not have been enough to fill the tank. I took a right at the blinking yellow traffic light and drove to the first diesel station I spotted. The place had a machine inside to convert my accumulation of spare change into cash, so I brought in all of what I had and turned it into nearly twenty dollars. It was after I returned to the pump that a strange old man resembling a cowboy shouted for my attention from the open door of the front seat of his truck. He had a massive but passive smile on his face.

"Now, you're a writer, aren't you?"

His West Texas dialect led me to mistake the word writer for *rider* and leave me unsure of his intentions. *How did he know I was a writer,* I thought to myself as I asked and learned that he wasn't talking about horseback riding.

"Now, you wouldn't happen to be looking for a place to stay for a few days, would'ya?"

I said that perhaps I was, but that I was more so looking for work and a path to a small sum of money to stay afloat with because he was looking at all I had. He speech was littered with metaphor, seemingly fixated on the meaning of life but finely so, like a veil concealing a blissful face. Each concrete word he chose hinted at something more.

"I have about 10 hours' worth 'a work, up at my land just five miles past town. Plenty of space for your bus, forty acres, water and power. You can settle in tonight and we'll start work in the morning tomorrow."

I thought carefully with the time I had in the moment and looked at him again before agreeing. I needed the money, and trusted my positive first impression of him. He had a short white goatee and a smile that showed his teeth, although what stood out the most were his black jeans tucking into fancy cowboy boots that revealed green and gold trimmed designs along them. I took note of this all in real-time, but in my head it wasn't his attire, nor his trusty smile that convinced me to accept the offer. His subtle references to the grand scheme of existence left me reminded of the Tao, the Blake quote from Naropa, and the eternal looseness that repeatedly appeared and departed with the waves of interaction that I chased after along the road.

Existence is one, or E Pluribus Unum, was his mantra, his main idea, his framework upon all else he spoke of was based off of. Of course I agreed—it was all there was, and regularly I had arrived at that conclusion at different points of my own trip of life.

32

The work went well, and the land was as picturesque as Buck first described it when I met him at the gas station. Pushed up and away from the edge of human development, his land was wild but essentially harmless, the elevation too high for rattlesnakes and with no history of bear encounters. He let nothing sharp grow from the ground, pulling everything but soft grasses that allowed my bare feet to press onto and pass along effortlessly.

When my ten hours of work ran up, we had made so much progress that he thought up more tasks to tackle and more work to offer me. From trimming trees to digging up protruding rocks, there were always things to do when the sun shined and I was willing.

His penname was Gmopond, but in conversation he went by Buck. Buck was impressively locked into a predictable routine that followed a daily cycle of maintaining his land, driving into town for lunch, and expanding his massive manuscript that by then had reached over 80,000 words. According to him, a vision brought him to Angel Fire seven years back, after he grew discontent with his beachfront property in Hawaii and sold everything he had only to retreat to the mountains and materialize his philosophical ideas that could no longer simply sit idly in his head.

I enjoyed the conversations he provoked as we worked. From the very beginning he spoke about his land in an odd manner. It was as if he was looking for a successor all along, someone to inherit and care for the land once he was done and through, and that perhaps I was he, the one he was searching for since arriving in Angel Fire and beginning his writings.

Undoubtedly we had met upon strange circumstances, but the bus frequently had that effect on people that I met spontaneously. I sincerely appreciated the quality of refuge that Buck's land offered, along with the wise words he shared with me when we worked. On off-days we drove to Taos, and even once down to Española for an appointment of his, trailing the Rio Grande as south as I had ever followed it, stopping frequently along the way.

In Taos, Buck introduced me to people from the mesa, one familiar street-side face at a time. His voice was free from fear and restrain in each interaction with them, even though he later confirmed the portrayals of mesa-dwellers that the hitchhiker once described to me. He knew the majority of the people we ran into in Angel Fire, and seemingly just as many when we went to Taos.

One day he brought me into an expensive, western leather shop with genuine hats, jackets, blankets, and rugs made of cow and buffalo. He bragged to the attendants that I was from New York as I admitted my amazement of their establishment.

As time went on, the work Buck had for me shifted from manual labor to editing the first book of his five-part manuscript. Once I agreed to do it, he had it printed, hole-punched, and entered into a 2-inch binder. For five days straight, I read and revised his work, flipping through the binder and filling each page with red pen markings and suggestions, really enjoying myself throughout the span of solitude and focus. I spent times of shade and darkness editing on the bus, and times of sunlight outside in a folding chair, binder in lap and pen in hand.

As each day passed, Buck's excitement for the book grew when we reviewed my progress. Sadly, his worries also grew simultaneously. Between editing sessions, I guided him through what I knew from my own experiences of self-publishing. I set him up with his own ISBN's, and offered my opinions in regards to the format of his cover art that he bought. I explained to him his rights in regards to copyright laws and regulations, detailing as much as I knew.

I made it clear that I was a deliberate avoider of automation and smartphones, and had my own mindful alternatives and preferences. Even though it was much easier for me to navigate and problem-solve on the internet than it was for him, I reminded him that it was of the least of my interest to spend lengthy hours clicking and scrolling. He understood this as I attempted to clarify my views, but as the days went on, he desired more and more internet assistance from me as he struggled to handle computer-work in any sort of timely fashion.

At this point, it had been over two weeks since the two of us met and he first brought me to his land. He had never had a visitor stay for as long as me, and struggled with the fact that not even his family would visit him, let alone consider inheriting his land for any reason other than to immediately sell it. From our very first conversation he mentioned his quest for a successor, and that talk only grew as I entertained it and didn't disappear. He didn't like to talk about this, but all along he expressed a distaste for the larger world that slightly but increasingly worried me. Unwilling to drink any water other than from his own land, what he said made sense but simultaneously left me wondering if his stressful paranoia was offsetting his healthy decisions.

Before I began editing his manuscript, I talked to him about Naropa and my interest in their eclectic program. He listened, but largely disregarded my excitement as I explained that I would soon be heading back up to Boulder for an open house event that I had gotten word of. The event wasn't for another week, but as it approached, he began to worry that once I left, I would never return.

I wanted to return. I didn't want to leave him with an unfinished book. That being said, his increasingly controlling and disapproving demeanor revealed to me a shortsightedness in him that I initially overlooked. How could he not see the benefits of me attending such an event? He understood from my explanations that Naropa was a scholarly literary institution, and that I looked to it highly in excitement to refine and build upon my developing skills. The problem may have stemmed from the broad viewpoint he had that all educational institutions simply miss the mark, and never taught him anything. To fix this, it was his dream to create his own institution, with free tuition and situated upon his land. He showed me the books that he wanted to base his courses on, which left me uncertain and suspicious of how his establishment would be any different than the corrupt ones that he scorned. I challenged him upon these remarks, especially because he could not see the value of Naropa that I described to him.

Up until the very Friday morning of my departure for the open house, I was under the impression that he was completely fine with my decision to leave for Boulder and return by Monday. The evening before, after I presented him with the binder full of my marks and suggestions, the two of us cleaned his small, spare cabin and rearranged the furniture after I spent the second half of the day painting the cabin's interior walls and ceilings. I decided to sleep in it that evening, keeping warm in front of the magnificent wood stove that was already necessary to enjoy Angel Fire's unfailingly cool September nights.

By then, I had already finished editing his manuscript. Combined with the frustration of flipping through the heavily marked pages along with noticing my proficiency at reworking the online version of his text document, he demanded that I stay, abandoning my plan to leave for Naropa, in order to help him continue editing.

I explained that I would be back in only a matter of three days, and that the open house meant so much to me and my long-term future. He only followed with projections of guilt, waving the future of his land and my own legitimacy over my head in a way that did nothing but push me away. As much as I enjoyed editing his work and learning from his wise words illuminating the essence of human connectivity, I could do nothing but start up the bus for the first time in over three weeks and head for Colorado.

33

Before I neared completion of the editing job and after grasping a rough idea of how long it would take me, we conjointly decided upon a flat rate of $500. As my time on the job surpassed fifty hours and I calculated my diminishing hourly earnings that I quoted him, I refrained from asking for more money and continued working on the manuscript until it was finished and I was proud of it. I knew that we could not call it the final edit, but I was sure and confident with what I had put into the work when I finally returned it to him.

The last thing I expected from him was discontent, but there I was, the morning of my scheduled departure, having to choose between the chance to finally meet and interact with Naropa faculty and throwing it all away in an effort to salvage my new friendship and acquaintance with Buck. He questioned my loyalty, doubting I would return, which came to me as a massive surprise. He worried for my well-being, unconfident that I could survive the city, leaving me with an ultimatum and choice to make. Initially only offering me half of the $500 we agreed upon, I expressed the disrespect that I felt and told him that it was time for me to leave.

Of course, I stuck with my decision to hit the road. I followed him to town with the bus, returning to the same gas station that introduced me to him. It already felt like months ago that we first met. He gave me the full amount that he owed me, $700, which included pay from other labor that we had not yet squared up on. I was parked at the pump when he approached me with the cash and handed it to me as I chatted with an elderly lady at a corresponding pump. In stoic fashion he said nothing to me as I thanked him and tipped my head forward. After he turned away and headed for the entrance of the station, I fueled up with a fraction of what he gave me. Then I walked over to his truck, pulled out his hidden spare key, opened up the front door, and left $100 dollars on his seat.

At that point, I found peace again, started up the bus, and left town.

34

Again in overwhelming recognition of the head-on thrills of unattachment, I watched Angel Fire disappear into my past and an old, familiar Colorado return. But before reaching Colorado, I took the business loop through Raton and impulsively stopped at a distinctive cowboy apparel store in search of a way to materialize a personal fresh start.

I left my old hat in the bus and entered the shop with a wild, loose head of hair.

"Awfully nice ride you have, assuming that bus out front is yours."

"An equally nice shop you have! You must get that a lot."

The bus was in sight through the large front windows of the shop, parked on the street, across two parking spots of Raton's main stretch of storefronts. The cowboy store was impressive with the moods it provoked from inside of me, raising questions in only a short time. Countless hats were on display throughout the store, aged ones with various degrees of ware and deformities, each with a small label and name next to them, each situated high and out of reach.

"I must ask, those hats up high aren't for sale, are they?"

The same lady that addressed me upon my entrance explained to me that the aged hats were not for sale, and in fact were donated over the years, many by family members of those deceased and some by the wearer of the hat itself. "Each hat has a story, tied to each owner. We've been gathering and compiling enough hats and stories to create a storybook of tales from the many generous hat-wearers."

I was intrigued. I explained without many details my desire for a new hat, a new start. It didn't take long for the helpful, good-looking lady to unite me with the hat I had unknowingly been searching for all along. Other than the fact that it took three tries to find one big enough for my head, I was immediately committed to the first style I chose. She asked me if I wanted the brim reformed, and that they offer to steam them to preference free with a purchase.

In the moment, I thought of the great Walt Whitman. The flat brim of his hat could not be forgotten as I complied and watched her begin to steam and reform the hat. Fascinating!

She wasn't quite satisfied with it after a minute or two of steaming, and asked if I was from the area. If so, I could return the next day and have it perfect. I replied that I lived very far away, but that I was not in a hurry and that I would happily come back after lunch to pick up the hat if that was enough time. Instantly, the new hat became my prized possession.

I returned after lunch with my old hat in hand. They were ecstatic to see it, excited to raise it among their wall of hats and add it to their collection of stories. I had only owned that old hat since the spring of that year, 2019, but had worn it for the majority of my days since purchasing it to the point that it was visibly discolored, disformed, and ready to be retired. The new one was an obvious upgrade, felt and magnificent, ready to accompany my many upcoming miles.

35

O continuous Colorado!
backpack full,
bus back in transit mode,
my compass not just a decoration again.
O freedom—nobody following,
nobody to follow but a path and a magnetic needle.

Welcome!

It was an enjoyable open-house—a rejoicing event of like-mindedness complete with inspirational words, inspirational actions, and inspirational gifts. Conversations with Naropa's president, Jack Kerouac School advisors, and other aspiring students left my heart full and assured that a like-mindedness did exist somewhere in the academic world.

     That night, after the conclusion of the event, I was so confident and happy to be in Boulder that I decided to attempt a return to an old hideaway that at the time seemed only a petty endeavor. I did not forget the dangers of such a cliffside, but I did underestimate the size of the parking lot and overestimate the off-road capabilities of the bus. I had only reached the place by Jeep back in 2017 on a road trip with Sam and Evan.

     Strangely enough, I am referencing Lost Angel. Maybe in a way I *was* a wandering angel up to that point, but I undoubtedly became a lost one when I attempted the toughest retreat the bus had ever seen. A climbing hotspot, Lost Angel was a popular destination for the rugged ones that offered free-camping if you could make it there. Free camping was nearly impossible to find in a city like Boulder, but became easier the further into the wilderness one was willing to travel.

The right-hand turn that diverged from the main road to Nederland was an intimidating one. There was a yellow sign warning of steep roadsides and no guard rail. The sign was not something to overlook, although I continued to believe that the bus would be able to handle it. It did, as I persisted, attempting to beat dusk and arrive before it was too dark and would become even more dangerous. I could feel the engine working excessively as I followed my memory to the climbing hotspot with breathtaking views and that feeling that you could die if you tripped on your shoelaces. Upon my arrival to the parking lot, the reality that the bus was close to half the size of the remaining, available space filled me with worry, but it was already too late and dark to turn around and head down. I somehow managed to clear a massive gulley and back into the only realistic spot that I could muster up. I had no other choice.

As I readjusted my wheels and attempted to reposition myself away from two other vehicles, the engine suddenly shut off when I was still in reverse. I was left with no option but to accept the spot I had nudged myself into.

As I pulled my parking brake and shut off the headlights, an angry camper immediately emerged from the trailhead.

"What do you think you're doing?"

I hadn't completely blocked in his van, but the length of the bus allowed him only a direct shot at the gulley if he wanted to leave. He immediately demanded

I leave or give him the space to drive around the gulley, but that was no option as the bus ceased to start or give any indication of operating capability. I didn't tell the man this right away, but he soon realized it after he gave me ten minutes to move.

When he did finally realize that the bus wasn't moving, he erupted. He tried to phone a sheriff or ranger, but had no service. An abandonment of his former plan to stay the night and leave early the next morning changed in an instant when he started up his van and aimed right at the gulley, smashing his bumper and momentarily getting stuck before a few more unpleasant sounds came from under his van and he drove away.

At that point I almost wished he did get through to a sheriff because I was utterly stuck with no idea what was wrong with the bus and no plan whatsoever to get it out. By then it was already dark, and the only complainer already departed, so I calmed myself down and prepared to deal with the task at hand the very next morning.

36

As soon as the sun shined through the bus windows I sprung up and began pacing around the bus. I began thinking up a list of options in my head. I was embarrassed by the park job I was stuck in, especially as campers soon began returning to their cars and packing up their gear. I peaked at them through the windows but did not yet draw my curtains open. A small group cooked breakfast on their portable stove. At first, I didn't even know what I could say to these people to help my situation, so I further retreated and brainstormed. Losing my cool, I turned to a page in my notebook and began scribbling a list:

Stuck atop of Lost Angel
--Make a deal and sell to stranger, scrap bus
--Hitch to town, buy batteries, get bus to start
--Tow to Trinidad
--Sell bus in town
--Try to jump batteries again

At that point it almost seemed that my best option was to put the bus in neutral and push it off of the cliff, as the thought of towing it was somewhere between a fortune and literally impossible. As I finished writing my list and brainstorming, I realized that I really had no hope but to pray that the bus was simply exhausted (like back in Kansas with Dibble) and needed a night of rest. I tried to turn the key again but nothing happened.

Once I gathered enough courage to begin talking with fellow campers and arriving day-climbers, my thoughts only sped up and continued hurrying through my head. I received miniscule support from the first interactions that I initiated, instead a sort of *good luck with that* reaction from multiple parties until finally a group of twenty-somethings broke the trend.

An average guy about my age appeared at the trailhead on foot while I was standing over the cliff and looking into the distance in deep thought. Only returning to the lot from their campsite to grab a few things from his friend's truck and head back into the woods, he assured me that he and his friends would help if I was willing to wait. Of course I accepted and thanked him before he nodded and trotted back down the trail.

I waited another hour before the group of four appeared with backpacks full of camping gear. They were shocked that the bus had even made it to the current place it was in. One of them had an electric jump-starter, which we connected to one of the three batteries in-loop and flipped the switch. After allowing it to charge for about thirty minutes, I tried turning the key again which resulted in a clean start! That is, until we removed the charger and the bus suddenly died again.

"Not sure what to do at this point, my man. Seems that your bus can't hold enough power without the charger connected."

I pleaded for the bus, by then in belief that it just needed a little more of a charge in order to hold until I could make it down the mountain. But upon another patient charge and attempt, the bus only repeated the action of starting until we disconnected the charger.

The driver of their truck offered me a ride to Boulder, but I wasn't ready to leave the bus and declined their gesture. They wished me luck, packed up their things, and left me alone in a parking lot that still had a few other parked cars which meant people in the woods who could maybe help, although there was nowhere near the same amount from that morning.

I continued deep, quiet contemplation. Out of the blue, no longer than an hour after the prior group left me, another truck pulled into the dirt lot and caught wind of my situation.

"Got any jumper cables?" I asked him, possessing just a little hope that a jump would do anything other than what the electric jump-starter could do.

This new guy was as confident as I was. We hooked up the cables to his truck, which clearly generated more spark than the prior. As we let it charge, we discussed my options, which were dangerous because if I attempted to drive away and the bus turned off abruptly again, I would probably be in an even more urgent situation in which the bus would be blocking at least five cars from exiting the lot. This coupled with the reality that an enormous gulley separated the bus from the exit, I hesitated but finally decided that if the bus were to start again and hold a charge, I would hit the gulley head-on and push for glory.

"You've got enough clearance with those tires— I wouldn't worry about getting over that ditch."

Upon removal of the cables and no indication that the bus would turn off again, I shook the man's hand quickly but diligently and made the attempt. Everything loose inside the bus leaped and quaked when I hit the ditch, but amazingly I cleared it and the bus just kept turning. I could not formally say goodbye or thank the man once the bus was in motion, but hearing his cheering and seeing his triumphant face in my mirror as I drove away sufficed and ignited my hope for the bus again.

37

The Mad Hatter of Denver
or at least he resembled,
also introducing himself as so.

He enjoyed giving,
kept handing me keepsakes
some of his dearest pocket objects—
"gold" timepiece
cigarettes, tweezers
wanted to pluck my eyebrows
hell no!

Brought me to Sox Place
hippie shelter.

There is a difference:
homeless and down
(bringing others down and oneself)
and homeless with a spirit
thrilled to share everything for all
willing to listen to everyone,
stopping for sincere interaction
—*conversation, anyone?*—
at every face.

He introduced me to his small crew,
guarding his fort (assembly of tents),
hilarious sidekicks.

Eventually I left him,
unwarranted but in good timing,
his trio of tents
pitched at the base
of a massive Denver cell tower.

Tents were a symbol of status
not all could afford or defend.
They scattered the shadows of Welton street
moving there in unison after a clear-out
of parallel California street
just two days prior.

The Mad Hatter knew each one,
and many more as we strolled along it.
Whacky at first glance,
a comrade at the second,
phoneless was he
but friendless he was not.

I assume, by now,
the figure has sauntered on
as I, like he,
drift ceaselessly
like a gust of wind
over grass.

Emerge   Exit

38

Rainforest, Bedroom

We expand and contract
to fit our living spaces,
spreading our things
when room is large
tightening when
spaceisshort—
as in narrow pages,
only partly dictating
my thoughts & breaths
but manifesting so differently
when there's simply more room.

The walls of this room
(like the pen I use)
leave marks, impressions.
If I leave anything up for too long,
unevenly the surface shades.
May I never leave
something tacked, taped,
or resting on a ledge
long enough to unevenly discolor the room
disturbing its unified form
when I step back.

O ceaseless Human connection,
to denounce is to divide.
If nothing else,
I celebrate the unexplainably simple

I heard about long ago
the untamed was not feared,
nature was not always exotic,

faraway,

before a split of primitive and cultivated

Choosing definitive, concrete,
and finally, industrial
it was all an illusion:
nature and us were always one.

The same groove
that otherwise constricts
those in stagnation
grooves the perfect nest

Freedom is a bluebird's perfect nest,
the biggest picture,

inner workings
grand unifying vital
simple

as the best sight is in-sight
the best café is the one at your corner

Trace the returning breeze—
as in a frosty draft,
the untamed inside may wither
rustling away until we seek it again

when losing relation,
unearth inner wildness

      it is there
      project it to the world

I am the one to care!
I recognize my workings
grand unifying vital
simple.

39

The successful life
is the successful idea
(and vis versa)
utter belief in action
restraint in mind
plain as day
completely

"Such a gypsy, me,
moving from room to room,
but how happy I am
to see you again!"

Lots of luggage,
a few foot-draggers ride the elevator with us
they ask her:
"How long are *you* staying?"

She wasn't a full-time gypsy,
only staying a few days,
but in her elderly self was a spirit,
keeping bright stories of her youth

After I carted up her luggage,
she asked one last thing.

"Can you help me connect,
get my tablet going?"

I tried but empty was the battery—
only a 0% memo on the screen.

All I wanted was to assure her

she was much more than 0%,
much more,
 "smarter phoneless—"

Thanks for that.

40

Calendar by bedside
blank, filling it in remembrance
recording events after they pass
rarely planning ahead
preferring to leave space to document

drawn with pen
assisted by ruler
colored sparingly with crayon
fill with most recent thought—

A land emerged
upon a turtle's shell
eagle watching over
weapons buried in dirt
white pine's branches
welcoming the unknown

this is the tree of peace,
Osoä'go:wah
green year-round,
land of love
(once was)

part three

TO FINISH SCHOOL

June, 2019

This is something I wrote and presented at the conclusion of Dr. Bob's seminar at SUNY Potsdam, which provided me with the final three credits that I needed to complete my degree.

There was an old lady, from the Cree tribe, named "Eyes of Fire", who prophesied that one day, because of the white mans' or Yo-ne-gis' greed, there would come a time, when the fish would die in the streams, the birds would fall from the air, the waters would be blackened, and the trees would no longer be, mankind as we would know it would all but cease to exist.

There would come a time when the "keepers of the legend, stories, culture rituals, and myths, and all the Ancient Tribal Customs" would be needed to restore us to health. They would be mankind's key to survival, they were the "Warriors of the Rainbow". There would come a day of awakening when all the peoples of all the tribes would form a New World of Justice, Peace, Freedom and recognition of the Great Spirit. (from Warriors of Rainbow Prophecy)

Native people in the Americas have been labeled as vicious savages almost immediately after the first settlers arrived from Europe seeking to "purify" and spread their beliefs to the new world. Could they have been more hypocritical? Early interactions with the natives revealed glaring technological differences between these clashing groups. These differences played a striking role in leading to the discontent and disgust that Europeans quickly attached to American Indians. Although the technological advancements of then are now vastly outdated by new systems, the quest to civilize and modernize is not over.

Corrupt officials continue to mislead the American public to this day, destroying precious land in trade for economic gains, leaving all humans at risk of suffering the consequences of environmental disregard. As the United States government successfully outlawed the right for local governments to oppose cell tower construction due to environmental or health concerns in 1996, it is evident that the fight to preserve what is sacred and essential for mankind's survival is still ongoing in the destructive fashion that has been plaguing this nation since the arrival of Columbus.

How have we gotten so far away from living simply and within our means, coexisting with the natural world? Violent conflicts between groups of people with contrasting viewpoints have plagued society for thousands of years, although in the grand timeline of human history, organized war is a relatively young concept.

Asking why these trends began is obviously a controversial, disputed upon question, although a few parallels in history exist from the period in which organized wars became the norm. For example, some believe that it was the agricultural revolution and the end of human migration that led to the separation of man from nature. As humans established themselves on plots of land and remained there, they began distancing from the natural world and convincing themselves that they are separate from the untamed wilderness. This ranking system is known as a totemic view of society.

Native Americans do not fear the untamed wilderness. This is impressively consistent across the many Indian nations, despite their great variety of cultures from nation to nation. They seem to agree that it makes little sense to hold irrational fears while immersed in primitive back country. When white settlers arrived, natives rejected this imported belief that there are "no friends to be made in the forest" (from NY Times review of Indian Country). Clearly, they are far from viewing the world totemically and had a hard time relating to Europeans that feared the unknown and pursued deforestation miles past practicality. Who are the savages, again?

With this being put forth, it is natural to wonder how the Europeans would ever coexist with other cultures that held such drastically different views regarding how a sacred way of life should be lived. Christopher Columbus immediately took note of the kindness of the first natives that he came into contact with, but feared being "Indianized" and destroyed them. Like other Europeans at the time, Columbus believed in the completeness of knowledge, and could not fathom that he had arrived on land completely unknown to the Old World. In comparing these new people to what he knew from Europe, he concluded that they were backward and dangerous. Perhaps the Arawak would have been spared if they had fancy technology when Columbus arrived, but the whites saw no church steeples or sharp metal swords and concluded that they must "modernize" or die (first encounters in the Americas article, facinghistory.org).

When white settlers realized that they could not destroy and replace all native people, they began resorting to relocation efforts and continuously pushing them around until many tribes were left with very little land that oftentimes could not be farmed efficiently enough to self-sustain themselves, leading to government dependence. But "to Navajo, to relocate is to disappear", and many tribes fought with all their might to resist white expansion and retain their traditional values (quoted from the film Broken Rainbow, 1985). Whites often confused natives with elaborate paperwork and ridiculous land leases that took advantage of their ignorance and left them poor and ravaged, depleted of resources that would sell for much more on the American free market once the natives signed away. Natives did not understand the concept of paying for land, and had no use for money that was offered for what was sacred. They were already rich, they believed, by inhabiting beautiful land and having all that they needed to sustain their communities while remaining in harmony with the landscapes.

When Tony and Sakohawiesere came into class to speak to us about their experiences as Native Americans, a student asked, more or less, what we can do as aspiring educators in search of amending what has been ripped apart since the times of Columbus. "It isn't about ideologies or politics. It's about the land," Tony said with passion. "It's about holding onto what we have left, and keeping it healthy and away from greedy fossil fuel companies and miners that look to deface it."

This runs true to this day, with examples of the Mohawk Conflict of 1990-91 and the construction of the Dakota Access Pipeline across sacred Indian land as instances of continued disregard for their land. What has been going on for hundreds of years continues as American officials look for profits and disregard the fragile landscapes that they seek to exploit. They use ignorance and corruption to grant themselves access to do so, keeping natives in the dark about the harms of radiation and the market value of non-renewable resources once they are pulled from the land. The Navajo nation could be the richest minority in the United States, but they are among the poorest, likely because of the deception that Washington has gotten away with (SUNY Potsdam class discussion 6/15/2019, also Indian Country in four corners chapter).

The natives are not the only ones at risk of suffering the consequences of our greedy, uninhibited deforestation efforts and implementation of "cutting edge" technology. Americans wrongly follow along with the belief that it is worth tearing down nature and building thousands of cell towers emitting radiation that we do not understand the long-term effects of, before the equipment can be tested and deemed safe.

If we have not already reached the point of no return, this is a subject in which we run the risk of taking it too far and causing irreversible physical damage to nature and ourselves. According to section 704 of the Telecommunications Act passed by Bill Clinton in 1996, local authorities can be sued for resisting the construction of cell phone towers due to perceived health effects. Is this not enough to question the authority and legitimacy of our massive government?

The plans to rollout 5G, the next generation of wireless technology, require a massive, dense network of cell towers placed close together and in close proximity to neighborhoods and communities, indoors and outdoors. They are called "small-cell towers", although they are not small, and in fact can be much larger than traditional telephone poles. They are made up of complex, bulky electrical equipment that emit radio frequency radiation (RFR) and millimeter waves that have been used in the past as a crowd control weapon which causes acute burning pain (Request denial of Verizon's small cell towers application article, emfsafetynetwork.org).

The research that the FCC uses for setting their standards of harmful radiation is vastly outdated and has been proven in peer-reviewed, published science as extremely harmful to nature (ant study, tree study). Many scientists believe it is the root cause of the dwindling bee population, and that many species of bird are at risk not only from tower collisions but also from the radiation emitted from these cell towers. RF radiation is increasingly being recognized as a new form of environmental pollution, although local governments and communities can be sued for opposing construction and implementation of cell towers due to taking health into account.

Research in this field can be difficult to obtain, as there no longer remains an unexposed control group. 5G technology is being pushed from the major cities to rural communities, under the reasoning that "everyone deserves the choice for affordable connectivity" (Supercharging Competition Wall Street Journal Advertisement, print, 4/13/2019). This holds true for the Navajo reservation, a nation with more than 15,000 homes that still lack electricity. The article cited regarding putting the Navajo Nation on the grid uses language like "they helped bring light to homes left in the dark for generations" and that "the rural electrification efforts aren't intended to push modern infrastructure on Navajo families, but rather to give them the same access enjoyed by residents in the rest of the country".

If there are clear scientific findings highlighting dangerous health effects of wireless technology, why would our government be racing as fast as possible to install these towers in every town in the United States?

Why are these scientific findings being swept under the rug and ignored?

Well, we are in a race with China and Russia for dominance over this modern technology, as Donald Trump banned Huawei amid the developing trade war with China. Huawei is China's leading manufacturer of 5G equipment, and number two in the world only behind Samsung (Forbes article on Huawei's popularity outside of the United States). Meanwhile, Huawei is being embraced by Indonesia, Saudi Arabia, South Africa, Turkey, and UAE (hidden backdoors Bloomberg article). On the other hand, Moscow already has "some 5,000 cameras installed with facial-recognition technology, and it can match faces of interest to the Russian state to photos from passport databases, police files and even VK, the country's most popular social media platform" (The Autocrat's New Tool Kit [ANTK] article from the Wall Street Journal, print, 3/16/2019).

As a matter of fact, this is already a reality in the United States. Much of this type of data is collected through automated microtargeting, which "relies on personality assessments to tailor content to segments of a population, based on their psychological, demographic or behavioral characteristics" (ANTK). This is supposedly what Russia did during the 2016 U.S. presidential election, harvesting data from Facebook in order to craft specific messages for individual voters based in part on race, ethnicity and identity.

When governments are in control of this massive database that continues to compile sensitive personal information about their citizens, imagine what they can do to spy, rank, and punish individuals who are deemed "unsafe" by their algorithms. As this technology advances, these algorithms will improve in accuracy and capability. In the United States, we collect and use this information "mostly for online advertising", as it is collected and utilized by private entities like Facebook and Google (ANTK) to serve specifically targeted ads and generate more revenue. We can only speculate if these companies share this information with Washington, although there is no doubt that it is at risk of falling into the wrong hands and used against citizens who otherwise assume their right to privacy.

To return focus to nations of indigenous people, I believe that it is them that hold the key to rising above the madness of this emerging "internet of things" that is being promised as 5G is rolled out and implemented nationwide. Groups like the Navajo stand as an example of a community removed from this technology, although the last corners of primitive, off-grid land are being threatened every day that communities are unable to fight back against this construction of hazardous equipment that has clearly made the majority of the world screen-obsessed. Manufacturers of 5G technology have already completed the installation of small cell towers on all major highways, urban zones, and now are pushing their way across rural towns and Native American territories and reservations.

Once these systems are completed and live, maybe we will begin to find closure regarding the true effects on our physical and mental health, along with our diminishing spirits. Until then, a grassroots community of rainbow warriors continues to quietly grow, exchanging knowledge, harmoniously connecting the ideals of elderly origins with the demands of the now for the sake of society, culture, and Earth.

Links to Cited Works

First Encounters in the Americas
https://www.facinghistory.org/holocaust-and-human-behavior/chapter-2/first-encounters-americas

Autocrat's New Tool Kit
https://www.wsj.com/articles/the-autocrats-new-tool-kit-11552662637

Commentary on the utility of the National Toxicology Program study on cellphone radiofrequency radiation data for assessing human health risks despite unfounded criticisms aimed at minimizing the findings of adverse health effects
https://reader.elsevier.com/reader/sd/pii/S0013935118304973?token=29A3E8E008C54C4300903F8AD0456A5F1E60F368A2EA10F43A6DE31A03A3414CB8D4C1DD57506C8127EC5CAF4581B4C6

Dumbing Down of the Ants
https://www.ncbi.nlm.nih.gov/pubmed/23320633

Huawei Fortifies #2 Spot in Global Smartphone Market, Beating Apple Again
https://www.forbes.com/sites/jeanbaptiste/2018/11/02/huawei-fortifies-2-spot-in-global-smartphone-market-beating-apple-again/#1b2482fc1305

International Scientists Against EMF:
https://emfscientist.org/index.php/emf-scientist-appeal

Local Governments Cannot Regulate
Environmental Effects of Cell Phone Towers
**https://www.honigman.com/media/site_fil
es/401_imgimgWeissA406289.pdf**
More Native American Prophesies related to the
rainbow:
**https://www.welcomehome.org/prophecy/
prophecies.html**
Scientists Warn of Serious Health Effects of 5G
**http://emfsafetynetwork.org/wp-
content/uploads/2017/11/Scientist-5G-
appeal.pdf**
Quality Review of Mathiesson's Indian Country
**http://movies2.nytimes.com/books/97/11/
23/home/matthiessen-country.html**
Radiofrequency radiation injures trees around
mobile phone base stations
**https://www.ncbi.nlm.nih.gov/pubmed/27
552133?dopt=Abstract**
Request denial of Verizon's small cell towers
application
**http://emfsafetynetwork.org/wp-
content/uploads/2018/05/Letter-to-Seb-
Verizon-5G.pdf**
Review of Section 704 of Telecommunications Act of
1996
**http://www.parentsforsafetechnology.org/t
he-telecommunications-act-of-1996.html**
Why Huawei smartphones are popular everywhere but
in the United States
**https://www.businessinsider.com/huawei-
smartphones-are-popular-all-over-world-
not-united-states-2018-12**

Warriors of the Rainbow Prophecy
https://upliftconnect.com/rainbow-prophecy/
"Rural Electrification Efforts" on Sacred Navajo Land
https://spectrum.ieee.org/energy/fossil-fuels/parts-of-the-navajo-nation-are-still-off-the-gridbut-thats-changing

Reader's Notes

Reader's Notes

About the Author

Sean P. Dwyer (b. 1995) grew up in Webster, New York. Dashing around during his summers off from college at SUNY Potsdam, he travelled to nearly all regions of the continental United States, including 46 states and more than 200 nights on the road.

In 2015, at the age of nineteen, he self-published his debut work: To Accept a Wooden Nickel: Perspectives of an American Hitchhiker. In 2018, he released Sometimes They Smile, an adventure book detailing his extended stay at Silver Spurs Ranch in southern Colorado.

Later in 2018, while in the opening stages of drafting Smarter Phoneless, an opportunity to purchase a school bus was presented to him and his friends. Their lease in Rochester, New York ended in May 2019, but with one week to spare he left again, this time with the bus.

By April 2020, Smarter Phoneless was ready. Looking forward, he has no intentions of discontinuing his travels or writing.

Made in the USA
Monee, IL
27 April 2022

95536101R00089